READ WHAT INFLUENTIAL PEOPLE ARE SAYING ABOUT THE BARON SON

"We learn the most important lessons of life from stories and fables. *The Baron Son* carries this tradition to a new height."
> —Brian Tracy
> Author of *Getting Rich Your Own Way*

"A great book to have if you are serious about furthering your career. I know what it takes to hit the top; this book is right on target. I love it, I love it."
> —Joe Girard
> World's #1 Retail Salesperson, as attested
> by the *Guinness Book of World Records*
> joegirard.com

"As a road map to wealth, power, and success, *The Baron Son* is an allegorical tale that is as powerful in its own way as *Who Moved My Cheese?*"
> —Al Ries
> Chairman, Ries & Ries, Inc.
> Co-author of *The 22 Immutable Laws of Branding*

"*The Baron Son* offers fundamental and understandable strategies for creating successful business executives and building wealth."
> —Arnold S. Goldstein, J.D., LL.M., Ph.D.
> President, Arnold S. Goldstein & Associates, LLC
> Author of *Asset Protection Secrets*

"Motivation to develop a healthy attitude for all aspects of life."
—Royce Gracie
Ultimate Fighting Championship Hall of Famer

"*The Baron Son* will enable you to identify core strengths and master areas critical to your success. It is one of the most effective methodologies I have encountered for developing self-mastery."
—Les Brown
Author of *Live Your Dreams*

"This book intrigued me from the moment I picked it up. It is truly enlightening and inspirational for anyone at any level. The refreshing and original approach is the most unique I have ever read in the field of motivational writing."
—Barry Kaye, CLU
Chairman, Barry Kaye Associates
Author of *Die Rich and Tax Free!*

"Through allegorical storytelling, Davis, Patterson, and Patton have accomplished what most business writers in today's market place have failed to do . . . create an exciting text that unlocks the secrets of wisdom, health, wealth, and happiness. After reading the first chapter, you will not only be hooked, but will understand why it is referred to as *Vade Mecum 7*—a resource to carry with you. A must-read for those who are truly interested in improving their financial position."
—Vi Brown
FY05 National President, Society of Women Engineers
Principal and Owner, Prophecy Consulting Group

va·de me·cum (vā-dē-'mēkəm) *n.*:
  a guidebook kept constantly at hand
  Origin: modern Latin, literal translation "go with me"

THE
BARON
SON

VADE MECUM 7

VICKY THERESE DAVIS

WILLIAM R. PATTERSON

D. MARQUES PATTON

Long & Silverman Publishing, Inc.
Las Vegas, Nevada

Published by

Long & Silverman Publishing, Inc.

800 North Rainbow Boulevard

Suite 208

Las Vegas, NV 89107

Visit our website at www.lspub.com

Printed in the United States of America.

Library of Congress Control Number: 2004090858

ISBN: 1–59575–357–5

Books from Long & Silverman Publishing, Inc. are available at quantity discounts for use as premiums, sales promotions, or in corporate training programs. For more information, please write to:
Director of Special Sales
Long & Silverman Publishing, Inc.
800 North Rainbow Boulevard, Suite 208
Las Vegas, NV 89107
Tel: (800) 99-LSPUB (57782)
Fax: (800) 77-FAXLS (32957)
E-Mail: sales@lspub.com

ACKNOWLEDGMENTS

This book has taken many years to complete. We would like to acknowledge the friends, colleagues, and family members who have supported us throughout the process. You are the true wealth of our lives.

To the fellow leadership and success strategists who have incorporated our practices.

To our friends in the National Speakers Association and Toastmasters International. Also to the program directors, agents, and speakers' bureaus, who requested our contributions to their causes.

CONTENTS

A WORD FROM THE PUBLISHER

Long & Silverman Publishing, Inc. discovers exciting works that reflect unique paradigms of thought. Helping clients grow their businesses and enabling individuals to achieve outstanding performance is our mission. We strive to tear down barriers and increase opportunities for dynamic authors with powerful messages. We pride ourselves in publishing materials that will contribute in meaningful ways to entrepreneurs, business leaders, salespersons, or anyone else desiring an advantage.

It is with utmost sincerity that we present you with a book we sense will change the lives of millions. It will prove an invaluable aid for principled individuals as they prosper. It intends to help its readers foster an economic system based on courage and abundance, rather than fear and scarcity. This text is meant for those who consider themselves "uncommon individuals," those not content to merely exist, but who desire to leave their mark on this world. This select group of individuals perceives what others miss. With superior tools and stratagems, they work more effectively than others. To many, when a lifetime of dedication bears fruit, it appears as sudden success. This is only because the casual observer does not see the underpinnings that motivated the achievement. *The Baron Son* clears the fog that hinders most, so that every person may have the methods to realize their goals. Hard work alone will not suffice. You must have the *proper* instruction to do the right things.

Two attributes are necessary for a person to reap benefit from this book. As its purchaser you have already exhibited both. The first is the desire to improve your circumstances; the second is the perceptiveness to seek out information that aids in the realization of that goal. Scores of individuals have accomplishments whose roots were planted from the reading of just one book. When this invaluable resource is treated as a study, the Supreme Principles will give clarity to your situation and provide you with unique ideas. *The Baron Son* will ignite the minds of a new generation of leaders and bring forth improved learning.

We all have the power to choose how we view the world. A limited perspective costs us a feeling of control over our lives. Without control, we are inevitably led to unhappiness. By selecting an empowering point of view, our opportunities become boundless. People will be drawn to you and will support your causes, and information needed to facilitate your success will be increasingly recognized. It is up to you to determine the impact you will have on the people you lead. The person you have in mind to become will be forged from the messages in these pages.

What is your calling? How might you deliver your greatest benefit to the world? Too often we dare not dream. We routinely offer justifications for a lack of time, for why our ingenious idea was never implemented, for why our funds are insufficient, or why we cannot align ourselves with skilled advisors. Upon completion of this study, these excuses will no longer suffice. Every day we read and watch the accomplishments of successful people and we ask, why not me? It is because you have yet to realize your full potential. See the promise within you.

FOREWORD

Some scholars believe that the written word is man's greatest accomplishment. Whether it actually is can be argued; however, it undeniably ranks high on the list of our achievements. The proper use of language to convey reason, which is what distinguishes us from our animal friends, has advanced humankind to become the sophisticated and accomplished leaders we currently are. Our ancestors have passed on to us history, tradition, life lessons, folklore, and other important messages via this medium, and we owe it to ourselves and future generations to continue this practice the best way we know how.

From the onset of writing *The Baron Son,* we were not trying to reinvent any wheels; we just wanted to supply an innovative approach. Yet, what should have been straightforward quickly became complex. Which principles to highlight and in what direction to steer our tale became a daily topic of conversation. Line by line, we argued over every detail. Like many others on a journey to success, we often saw the sunrise during the process, which from inception to its realization on the following pages, took nearly five years and a lot of phone calls. Utilizing the art of negotiation with each other, the publishing company, and everyone else on the path to seeing our vision realized, we forged *The Baron Son* into this finished work. We understand that we all must do whatever it takes to become financially adept—anything that will make the lessons stick. So we try different approaches, attack from different angles, because what matters with financial education is breaking through to everyone, from the homeless to those with multiple homes. After all, a life is a life; each one deserves to be enriched. With this addition to financial and personal libraries, we have repackaged the life lessons that need to be addressed, and have hopefully done so in a way that is palatable for everyone.

Americans of every economic class can tell you what celebrity is dating another. We know the latest fashion trends, the newest diet, and the slickest car. We invest in relationships at our respective places of business, yet many of us do not understand how to invest in the businesses themselves. We hope that with the release of *The Baron Son,* even more of those individuals, who previously thought they had no reason to read a business book, will find themselves mistaken. Once you complete the first chapter, you'll be well on your way to a lifetime of successful investing. You will foster fantastic relationships with your colleagues who also read it. And you might even find yourself encouraging others to get on the bandwagon. It doesn't hurt for children to start picking it up, too.

So, what are you still reading this for? Flip to page one already! Get ready to be entertained—and maybe even enlightened here and there!

THE BARON SON

THE IRRESISTIBLE FORCE

n the days of yore there lived a man known solely as the Baron. Persuasive in demeanor, he had a charisma underpinned by life's experiences. His rational temperament left him disinclined to submit to convention. He was prudent as a man could be; even the most learned of sages coveted his infinite wisdom. As the richest, most influential man in all Mh'ki, the Baron was respected by all who knew of his qualities.

Upon the third dawn of each week, the Baron could be found in the study of his vast palace. The earthen walls and ceiling were inlaid with diamonds strategically placed to display the heavens' many constellations during torchlight hours. The Baron preferred the effect at sunup, when eastern light would fill the room, casting millions of tiny prisms all about. Settled upon sumptuous cushions of rare furs, he would hold a lotus position in the room's center whilst deliberating over the contents of his oft-referenced scrolls. This was how Wali, his aide, came upon him one morn, abruptly curtailing the Baron's concentration.

"Pardon the intrusion, my lord. Three figures approach on foot from the east. Art ye expecting company?"

Brows furrowed, the Baron nimbly rose from his seat and walked to the window. There he observed three shaded forms in the distance, the sun rising at their backs. Intrigued, he ordered Wali to halt their progress and make certain of their intentions. Wali nodded in obeisance and parted hastily, then called upon two sentries to saddle up their steeds. The Baron watched as his auxiliaries charged on horseback, kicking up golden sand with each fierce stride whilst the strangers continued their advance toward his estate.

Two hundred paces from the intruders, Wali drew his gleaming scimitar from its scabbard. He motioned for them to cease their course, and the men had a brief word. Wali insisted they hold their positions, then he returned to the grounds to report.

When in the presence of the Baron, and slightly out of breath, Wali announced, "Three men, having journeyed days, are resolute in speaking directly with you, my liege."

Still facing the window, the Baron questioned, "Dare they be so bold as to approach mine estate with no word of their forthcoming?" He paused briefly as he thought of a solution. "Since they thought it wise to venture uninvited and without warning, so be it," he said. "Fetch and place them before me, that I might elicit their request." He finally turned to Wali and added, "Make them wait in the drawing room, for I shan't allow them to disrupt my daily meditation." The dutiful servant bowed and left the Baron to carry out his daily regimen.

Wali escorted the wayworn men into the Baron's domain. They were ordered to wash themselves free of grime and don the fragrant oils and fresh robes provided them. Wali led them to the receiving area off the main hall where he instructed them to wait. When the guests entered the antechamber, their eyes widened in awe of what they beheld. The room was decorated with intricate tapestries depicting pastoral scenes and ornate designs that stretched the height of the walls. Inhabiting each corner were bowls of exotic flowers commingled with tropical fish in pools of water. Soft billowing fabrics of green and gold gently caressed the air as wind blew in from the large picture window at the room's center. It was a welcoming scene for the three outlanders after having trekked for days in the unrelenting heat and torrid sands of the Bunzir Desert. Having seen nothing but the vastness of barren land that stretched before them, they were awakened by the vibrant colors and activity. The guests enjoyed the breeze whilst they tarried for what seemed an eternity as the Baron carried out his activities.

Upon the conclusion of the Baron's obligations, daylight had already begun to fade. Wali acknowledged nightfall by lighting candelabra in the alcove. The three strangers obediently stood in the corner. Tongues of flame illumined their drooping faces, causing Wali to snicker to himself as he continued to light more candles. Shortly thereafter, the Baron entered, invigorated by his evening meal. He was dressed in resplendent robes of knitted cashmere the hue of camel hair, which guarded against the chilling nocturnal winds that blew furiously in those lands.

The Baron studied his guests intently, taking notice of the heavy satchels at their feet and their youthful faces. They appeared weary after standing in wait the greater part of the day. Amused, the Baron ordered Wali to bring in seats. Poised

at attention in the corner of the room, Wali directed footmen
to arrange silken cushions in an arrangement that faced the
Baron to the entrance and the young men to their host. As in-
conspicuously as they had entered, the footmen ushered
themselves out of the antechamber to leave the Baron with his
visitors.

The master of the house took his seat, then extended his
hand for the guests to rest their feet as well. When they had
positioned themselves accordingly, the Baron's solemn stare
dared each one to initiate his appeal.

"Most honorable lord," remarked the boldest, "I come
before you in the righteous name of Tunde. We three hail
from Hamaada, where your mark is legend. Understanding
your time to be precious, we request an audience of you because ye art clad in robes of majesty, your name honored in
far-off lands; ye art the man whose wealth bests any other in
the history of life. We have come for your holdings are vast,
proving your knowledge to be immeasurable. Confuse us
not, my lord; we seek not your gold, but the wisdom that
birthed it."

Devoid of any apparent emotion, the Baron elected not
to reply.

Trying his best to mask the nervousness in his voice,
Tunde continued, "In exchange for this wisdom, we have
brought gifts, for one mayeth not reap recompense without
sacrifice. As such, we offer up our most significant possessions that have been passed down from father to son, in exchange for what we will grow to be. We beseech your acceptance, fair Noble, for denying us would leave us no recourse
but to demonstrate our perseverance. We possess the ability
to endure the hardships of the path that lies before us. Our resolve is akin to the trickle of water that in time becometh a
raging stream carving stone."

Upon the close of his address, the youth produced from his satchel a heavy shield with his family crest branded on its plate. It had been presented to his family by the king of Hamaada ages ago, in commemoration of his forefather's performance in battle and dedication to the people. Tunde gazed upon the heirloom with pride and laid it at the Baron's feet. Eyes lowered, the next young man by the name of Khaleef, stepped forward and bestowed upon the Baron the staff of a shepherd, made of ebony wood and tipped with a silver cap in the shape of a ram's head. It had been crafted five generations ago by his forebear and had since been passed down to each firstborn son destined to inherit the family trade. Mbolaji, the third gift bearer, offered a decorative box that when opened, played music from a space hidden by a wooden partition. His father, a renowned artist, had created this treasured piece.

"What would cause you to think my wisdom worthy of such esteemed gifts?" queried the Baron.

"The charitable works ye hast endowed upon many lands have merited an honor much more precious than our offerings. Such bequests shall not go forsaken by the heavens," said Tunde. "We trust these gifts shall warrant us a similar consequence."

The Baron pressed, "What strides of your own have ye taken to acquire this knowledge?"

"We have prepared ourselves as best we could for the time when we might appeal to you. Laboring days and nights, we have studied the laws that govern wealth acquisition, but our reading hath left us empty. Scrolls do not speak back, most honorable lord, nor do they contain the experiences ye hast successfully navigated."

The Baron's approval of the petitioner's response was evident. "For such young men, ye exhibit the wisdom of those who have seen many a moon. I might take you for my pupils, on the condition that ye hold three promises sacred." He paused to note a sudden exuberance lift the faces of his inquisitors. "On the first hand, never lose faith in the teachings of your enlightener. On the second, ye are not to squander your breath in teaching this wisdom to those who demonstrate not the desire nor fortitude to learn. Finally, that ye are never to live discordant to the teachings, regardless if your days bring joy or hardship."

The youths honored the covenant with the Baron and eagerly took their seats. "We thank you, noble benefactor," they acknowledged.

"There will be moments when my manner of instruction might strike you as remedial. 'Tis during these times I wish you to be all the more attentive. Do not underestimate austerity, for therein lie truths men have sought for ages," the Baron proclaimed. "The unaware seek verities cloaked in mystery. Those with aptitude seek truisms that utilize words understood by most, if not all. If 'tis left misunderstood by the masses, 'tis undoubtedly an inferior perception." The students thirstily absorbed this teaching, hunching forward in their seats the better to hear him. "Discuss my views collectively; bring only refined thoughts before me. Thoroughly learn your lessons to prepare the foundation in which the seed of your ambition might be planted."

"Yes, Enlightener. We wholly desire your tutelage and avow our commitment to truth in action," said Khaleef, the frailest and shortest of the three visitors.

"If ye wish the education to produce great wealth, ye must have definite purpose and a desire that burn with the intensity of a flame," the Baron declared as he pointed to the burning wick of one of the patchouli-scented candles.

He shifted in his seat and leaned forward as if ready to rise. "Understand, this cornerstone principle hath brought me profusion in myriad forms and created wealth for multitudes of men. All things in my possession have stemmed from this truth. Let us inhabit more comfortable quarters. I shall recount to you the story of mine own definite purpose, which hath awarded me such abundance."

* * *

I am the sole heir of a man called Qahhar of Shem. My mother died giving me life; Father never remarried. He was a noble in the king's court. The nobles were skilled plenipotentiaries and guardians of the king's treasury. They spent their days studying the laws of wealth, attempting to transmute base metals into gold, and preparing elixirs of longevity. 'Twas said they generated riches from ash and built vast empires with mere thought, their knowledge was so expansive that pieces of silver multiplied without physical labor.

One day Father and his superior, Adnan, were in the midst of their collection itinerary for the king. They traversed the territory with a regiment of soldiers, gleaning tribute from the townspeople. Whilst they rode, Adnan made mention to Father of his contentment.

"The nobles' teachings have brought understanding of the Laws of Gold and much wealth to my coffers. It hath kept my stomach full and made for libation aplenty. I bear no sympathy in mine heart for the paupers of this land; theirs are the thoughts of serfs. They deserve the poverty that plagueth them as would a contagion."

"Adnan, hath not your appreciation for the blessings allotted you by the heavens developed any compassion for the plight of your brethren?" challenged Father, bewildered.

"Nay, Qahhar, it hath not. I acquired much when little was to be had. 'Twas I who sought food when my paunch ached from hunger, potables when my cup flowed not, knowledge when callowness and imprudence dominated my days. However, the peasants seek not knowledge, only merriment. Time and again they elect immediate gratification over wiser exploits. They seek not the Way, only stability in complacency. Nor do they seek wealth, nay, merely survival. They were born servile, and as such they shall perish. Pay close attention, brother. I shall open thine eyes to my sincerity upon our first collection."

Father and Adnan stopped at a papyrus shop operated by a comely woman, her crippled brother, and her adolescent son. Adnan barked harshly at the woman, "Where is thy tribute for the king?"

"Please spare me, my lord, for my purse is unfilled. The season hath left mine harvest thin. We have but few goods; all the territory hath fallen on hard days. Our stock remaineth unpurchased, and gold cometh not."

Adnan said, "Mine ears are incapable of hearing such defeatist words. Thy king careth not of the problems of a papyrus merchant, nor shouldst thou project thy lack unto those who must carry out his command. Thou hast occupied his territory, lessened its yield, and missed two payments. As such, thou hereby forfeitest thy freedom and material possessions, which shall serve to benefit the throne." The nobleman commanded three nearby soldiers, "Take her to the palace!" Then he turned to his companion and asked, "Qahhar, dost thou still not see the truth of my words? They all seem to have one rationale or another for evasion, do they not?" Father was taken aback at Adnan's ruthless display.

Adnan instructed two guardsmen to claim three quarters of the woman's chattel as tribute and apportion the remainder amongst themselves. As she was ushered from her storehouse, the woman tore free from her captors and fell to her knees. She tugged Adnan's robes, begging that he grant them more time. Caddishly, he spat curses and struck the woman. Adnan snarled, "How darest thou sully the garb of a noble!" Before he could deliver another blow, Father restrained him.

The young boy ran up to defend his mother, but was stopped by his crippled uncle. Adnan gave the order to have them all taken as indentured servants. Overcome with sympathy, Father engaged his senior in an effort to show the boy and the impaired man mercy. "Wise Adnan, would not a senseless boy and a halt man only burden our king, consuming more room and board than providing labor?" With much reluctance, Adnan agreed and spared the two.

Father extended his hand to the woman and gently lifted her from the ground. "What is thy name?"

"Laiqah," she whispered.

"My lady, albeit the backs of thy brother and child were spared, the law requireth thee to serve the king to absolve thy debt."

"Bless you, Noble, for your show of mercy in sparing my family. Everlasting shall my gratitude be. I will comply with the law, although unjust."

Adnan called, "Take her into custody!" The soldiers obliged with great haste.

As Father and Adnan left the shop to resume collections, a pack of youths approached them. One timid boy queried Adnan, "Could it be possible one day to grow and be a lord the likes of you?"

A terrible laughter rose from the regiment of soldiers. Adnan barked, "Ignoramus, dost thou not know that thou art but a mere serf? There will be nothing for thee but burdensome times, hunger, nakedness, and out of doors. Make way, fatuous child!"

As the soldiers trotted away, they chortled at the expense of the peasant boy. Father hung his head, uneasy with Adnan's coarse tongue and show of force. His commander smirked at him. "Thy spirit hath become female. Dost thine heart bleedeth for such a laughable simpleton?"

Father dared not reply. Adnan's provocation was a trap of which he was all too aware. Thus, they returned to the palace without another word betwixt them.

Later that evening Father paced to and fro in his quarters. The events of the day prompted him to reflect on his nobility in disgust. When he retired to bed, he stared into the ceiling, calling into question the ways of the nobles and laws of the king. Was his own conduct righteous, or was he destined to become a reflection of his cohorts? These contradictory thoughts conjured in him a motive to act in discordance to the throne, albeit to do so would constitute treason. Equally, not to act on an impulse that plagued him so strongly would be sedition against what Father held true.

'Twas in that moment he realized that to abscond was his only remedy; to stay in the province meant that his thoughts would remain his own, yet his actions would betray his heart. Are not these the toils of prophets? But what could he do for his brethren? He was but one voice, zealous to relay life-altering messages to those in search of the truth.

The following day Father visited his old friend, Ikleel, and divulged his plans to leave the realm to teach the Laws of Gold to anyone who wished to learn them.

"Thou hast observed as have I, that the actions of the nobles are contrary to the will of the people, and being such, cause thy brethren grave hardship," Father said. "The path of thy king will destroy thy people, and eventually the empire. Note the territory, for instance. He useth the resources of the land to fight unjust wars, further depleting our wealth. An increasing number of merchants have gone insolvent, and people have not the gold with which to procure medicine or food." He paused to check their surroundings for eavesdroppers, then resumed. "Thou art aware that when the common man prospereth, so shall the king in turn. When his people suffer, inevitably so shall he. 'Tis the eyes that deceive the king; he sees scarcity as abundance. He understandeth well the Laws of Gold; great wealth could easily be granted to all who reside under his governance. Yet in the mentality of this Barmecidal king, to share the Laws would risk his wealth."

Father stopped, clutched Ikleel's shoulder, then earnestly looked at his friend whilst preparing to petition the unspeakable. "For one to contemplate leaving the kingdom to teach such laws is sure to invite death. Ikleel, upon heeding my words, wilt thou risk thine head in this effort alongside me?"

"Fear not, for mine heart weigheth just as heavy," Ikleel remarked in a solemn tone. "Thou hast felt the burden of the rapacious acts conducted by thy fellow nobles for some time, and if one shan't die for a cause so valiant, one deserveth not the breath to witness the sun give birth to another morn. Qahhar, thou art a man of honor and hast proven courageous and virtuous through thine every course of action. I place my trust in thee, and dare travel at thy side no matter the cost. Whether by my life or my death I enlighten the world, so shall my fate be."

Father sighed in relief and smiled in thanksgiving. He credited Ikleel's bravery. "I shall make preparations and gather our scrolls. See to it that men are secured for the journey. Thou must exercise the utmost discretion, for our designs must never reach the court's ears."

The following sunrise, Ikleel visited several nobles at their estates regarding Qahhar's appeal. They all requested more time to consider the proposal. He then approached a few elder nobles who said they wished to help, but they seemed insincere. Such a mission surely would be the death of Father; by offering their assistance, they too would face the blade.

"Indeed, we are privileged old men, having lived long and fruitful lives," one of the elders proclaimed. "But this day is not fit for dying, nor shall the morrow be. We shan't desire that our fate be met in such a fashion. As our stories are told in the scrolls of the court, betraying our king would bringeth no glory to our heirs. They might celebrate our lives for a day, but for all others, we think not."

Several days passed. Ikleel reported to Father that he entreated nobles who refused to turn against the throne.

"They fear the loss of privilege their positions afford. Even in their hearts, if they felt as we, such disloyalty is considered nonsensical. One would carry the risk of finding oneself with neither the support of the populace nor the court. It hath been said that the people would never unite with thee, for they will not fight for that of which they possess no knowledge. Thou shalt fail to conscript nobles. These men have much to lose and less to gain. Attempting such a seemingly futile endeavor certainly would amount to a most unsavory demise."

"Evidently they stand not for justice. What is more," Father noted, "we now must expedite our plans, for our security hath surely been compromised."

When Adnan was informed by one of his spies that Father planned to leave his post, he quickly notified the king and called for Father's incarceration. At dusk, the king conferred with his council in the assembly.

"We shall smite this faction of traitors with one decisive blow. Take the heads of Qahhar, as well as those of his family and anyone whom he solicited. They have withheld their tongues from warning the Crown. Such treachery meriteth death," dictated the king.

"Your Highness, those numbers might be inestimable," rebutted Adnan, standing up from the third row of men.

Upon rising from his throne, the king reasoned, "The greatness of their number implies a threat equally proportionate. Do as I command!"

Adnan departed from the meeting and was met in the corridor by the leaders of his regiment. He gave the order to swiftly seal off all possible routes of flight from the Yunanti territory.

One of Adnan's lieutenants inquired, "What hath made the king so brutal? Slay innumerable townspeople and nobles alike?"

Adnan responded with a question of his own. "Couldst thou rest at night in the midst of treachery?"

"Nay, I too would be disquieted with such a dilemma pending. How dost ye propose to know which nobles suppressed notice of a conspiracy?"

"I dare not propose. Massacre them all. Best I err for the sake of caution and advance mine own station in the court than allow a traitor to live. I wish not to seal mine own fate. Prudence would suggest a precise course of action, thereby removing any possible threat."

The lieutenant eyed him in envy of his decisiveness. "A most discerning pronouncement."

Adnan resumed, "Conceal thine intentions well. Let it be heralded amongst the nobles that a celebration in their honor is to be held. Make it known to their loved ones that they too should attend . . . at the behest of the king himself. Talk of this as a celebratory affair for all who are deemed associates of noblemen. Then we shall confine everyone, and before the sun riseth seven times there will no longer be dissent within the kingdom."

Laiqah, now one of the king's bondservants, was scrubbing the gray stone floor on her hands and knees in the same corridor in which Adnan and his lieutenant spake. Whilst finishing her cleaning obligations, she overheard their plans as they passed. The moment when opportunity presented itself, Laiqah scurried off to locate Father and send word to her brother. He was the only man of the throne who had ever shown her mercy; she felt it only right to repay his gesture.

Having risked her life throughout the arduous day, she finally tracked Father down. Laiqah pleaded for him to retire from sight, lest he suffer a most horrible fate.

"Noble Qahhar, seek out my brother, Vasu, whom ye spared in my shop that day. I have already sent him word to harbor you from those tyrants."

"Thank thee for thy benevolence, Laiqah. 'Tis now I who am in thy debt."

Father visited with Ikleel and told him of the breach.

Ikleel began to apologize, "Forgive me, I—"

Father stopped him midspeech. "Occasion might arrive when thine apology shall be necessary, yet do not misstep and take this as one of them. Besides, we have not the time. 'Tis already done."

"What of the nobles? Do we not owe them warning?"

"How wouldst thou propose we distinguish whom, or how many, have broken faith with us?"

"I could not be sure, Qahhar."

"We can bear no more risk. We must comport ourselves as if the lot betrayed us and speak with no one; this journey is to be ours alone."

Shortly thereafter, Father came home with a look I had never before seen. 'Twas as if a cloud had shrouded his face in melancholy. I was overcome with a distinct sense of foreboding when I gazed into his eyes. He told me, "Thy father hath chosen a path that will endanger the lives of all dear to him. Prepare thyself, my son, for tonight we flee under a cloak of twilight."

Whilst I gathered my few belongings, a man in princely robes silently appeared in mine unlit quarters. Startled, I instinctively drew my scimitar and demanded, "Which art thou, friend or foe?"

"I am Nasir, a friend . . . thy guide," he whispered.

"Nasir? Where's Fa—?"

"Speak not! Scarce moments of freedom remain. We must flee with urgency," said the stranger.

Befuddled, I amassed only what I could carry with ease and took leave, following closely behind mine escort. As we entered the quadrangle, I noticed Father and Ikleel crouched at the far end, in the shadows of several pillars. Mine heart pounded in suspense. As we made our way, I dared not whisper, lest it was the blade for which I longed. The king's garrison stood within earshot, surrounding the courtyard.

"The king would expect an escape through the gates, so we shall go over the wall," Father deduced.

Father and Ikleel forcibly subdued nearby members of the garrison. After their brief tussle, we swiftly rappelled the palace walls and boarded a small raft Ikleel had concealed in tall grass earlier that day. With it, we traversed the river downstream. We later jettisoned the shoddy raft and betook ourselves afoot for what seemed an infinite number of paces until we reached town.

'Twas in Laiqah's despoiled papyrus shop that we found Vasu, who greeted us with nourishment and shelter.

Father offered Vasu a humble smile. "We are appreciative for thine aid." Conscious of his host's physical limitation,

Father embraced him gingerly. "We shall remain out of sight a fortnight; spies are certain to be ubiquitous. Once Adnan giveth up the hunt, we shall commence teaching."

Seven suns rose and set, and on the eighth day the king's men posted word about the public execution of duplicitous court members. It was to take place by the gloaming. Since it was still much too dangerous for Father to appear, Vasu went to observe in his stead. Later that eve, he returned with his account.

"Never have I seen such fear in my brethren. The noble Adnan oversaw the executions, all the while proclaiming 'No one is above the laws of the king, including his court.' 'Tis disheartening when a king findeth it fit to kill scores of men and imprison their families."

I inquired of Father, "Why would the king incarcerate women and children as well?"

"His purpose was twofold. To instill fear in the masses, insuring they would never rise against the throne. Also to guarantee that no one would be able to avenge his or her father or husband. Thine own freedom is in peril, my son, and if ever discovered, thou surely wouldst befall a similar fate."

I understood the gravity of Father's words. From that day forth, I was conscious of the potentially fatal consequences of mine actions.

Three moons came and went, seasons changed, and Father was eager to begin teaching the Laws of Gold. He gave Vasu coins from his satchel. With this newfound wealth, Vasu paid quittance against tariffs owed, reopened the papyrus trade, and built an addition to house Father's school. Vasu told whoever should inquire that he had found prosperity gambling in a region far from theirs. Since he was a known speculator, it raised little suspicion amongst the king's subjects. Some applauded his newfound good fortune, making an allowance for the lack in his physical condition. His handicap seemed to win him favor in situations where unimpeded men gained no sympathy. For most it merely held true that prosperous and debilitated was the far better life when compared to capable yet insolvent.

The school's attendance grew rapidly. Partisans spread throughout the town, and soon Adnan was made aware that Father was alive and teaching the Laws of Gold. Not long after, Father's destiny was settled. The king mounted a full-scale assault on the school with instructions that it be burned to the ground with Father bound inside.

The same day, Father sent Ikleel and me for provisions. Upon our return, we found both the school and store consumed by flames. Dozens perished in the blaze; no one could have survived.

"I must try to contain the fire!" cried Ikleel.

"Ikleel, ye cannot expect to return from such a blaze! All hath long since turned to ash!"

"Thy father and I sacrificed all for this cause. I owe him and the other martyrs an effort to save what I can or join them in mine attempt."

'Twas with those words that Ikleel disappeared into the conflagration.

I dropped to my knees and began to sob. 'Twas then I felt a hand grasp my shoulder; 'twas Nasir. With tearful eyes and contempt on my tongue, I lamented, "What am I to do? Having lost everything I cared for, I am left with nothing!"

He asserted, "One hath the freedom to do whatever thing only when all hath been lost. Therein lies the need to select one's proper route."

Disturbed by the severity of the situation, coupled with Nasir's seeming lack of compassion, I belted, "What course dost thou speak of? I see not a path!"

Nasir said, "Hear me well. Thine home, loved ones, and position of nobility are no more. Thou must choose a purpose for thy life. Courage is a prerequisite to initiate this journey; dedication, another to consummate it. Peasantry is an option, however I shan't endorse such a despondent resolution. If I were to remain with thee, we might erect a kingdom that reaches the heavens. The decision is thine alone. No other may sift one out in thy stead. I could provide thee with an arsenal of knowledge, but to make best use of thy potential, thou oughtest be staunch about that which thou desirest. Weigh these words prudently, then elect thy definite purpose."

"I know not how one decideth one's mission. Wherever would I start?" I questioned Nasir from behind a curtain of tears.

He aided me to my feet and dried mine eyes with the sleeve of his robe. Nasir tutted then spake, "Consider every option and have not fear in thine heart nor thoughts of failure. Only then can it be asked, What will I do?"

"I would complete what Father began and teach the people the Laws of Gold."

"Thou hast witnessed the consequences of that action." Nasir masterfully paused. "The king will come for thine head within six moons . . . Now, dost thou still wish to teach?"

"Yes," I replied. I wiped my face and straightened my posture whilst making this vow. "I would impart the knowledge to even more people than Father did, so the chance it mighteth survive would be all the more probable."

"Dost thou not know self-preservation? What dost thou hold valuable?" inquired Nasir.

"I was taught that value lies in kinship, prosperity, and liberty." As we walked away from the fire, I found myself fully engrossed in my declaration and less focused on my loss.

"My mission shall be to give the masses the tools necessary for empowerment. Also, to create the self-sustaining might within them to realize their aims."

"What wouldst thou need to accomplish such a mission?"

"Insight the likes of an oracle, persistence like that of water, and the patience of the earth." I stopped and faced Nasir. "It hath come to my notice that definite purpose and fervor are to be prescribed, with unshakable confidence mutually important. The ability to create benefit for others and act decisively have proven fruitful; the wisdom to learn from failure, even more so. Father proved these. I would need the aid of men wiser and more talented than I, as well as the means to multiply beyond that which is attainable by mine own efforts. Notwithstanding, compassion for my brethren and an understanding of self encompass all these qualities."

* * *

The young men hung on every word of the Baron's tale. Although exhausted, they pleaded for the lesson to continue.

"'Tis enough for one day. Debate the significance of definite purpose. If ye are able to prove it false, demonstrate it for me upon the morrow."

Wali escorted the pupils to their quarters. In parting, he reinforced that they continue to explore their thoughts of definite purpose and desire into their slumber. "Next to your mats, ye shall find clay tablets. Etch your definite purpose upon them and read it aloud for daily affirmation."

As the young men prepared to rest, they resumed conversation from their mats. Tunde, a youth of average height and lean proportions, reasoned, "One's chosen mission and the will to bring it into existence comprise one's irresistible force. What are thy thoughts, Mbolaji?"

Mbolaji, a man of imposing physical stature, became excited by such lateral thinking. "One must selecteth the proper thoughts and cultivate them so that they mighteth flourish. One should be forever heedful to till one's mental garden, and learn to do so unconsciously. To boot, one needeth prepare a sensible plan. Continue, Khaleef, please."

Staring up at the night sky through a window, tired yet unable to prune the newly cultivated thoughts coursing through his mind, Khaleef felt compelled to add, "In one's heart and mind, one should birth a rightful purpose, making this intention the focus of all thoughts, and actualize it. This goal should hold utmost priority, and one should provide it with the commitment it deserveth, without surrendering one's thoughts to diversions.

"To rest at night with thoughts centered on one's purpose and desire cause the mind to utilize the picture it hath been given, in the same manner that the stonecutter relieth on his plans. One's planted thoughts sculpt the actions of one's waking hours for the attainment of one's aim. Let us retire to better prepare a stronger foundation on the morrow."

THE INVINCIBLE SHIELD

The three pupils awakened, eager to continue their lessons. The account from the previous night reverberated along the walls of their minds as none other had before. When Wali went to rouse them, he was astonished to find the students already bathed and robed, patiently marking time in their quarters. At Wali's behest, they followed as he turned to lead them through the grounds. The winding bends through the tortuous labyrinth caused them to lose their orientation; it seemed an impossible path for anyone to remember. Finally, the quartet came upon an ornate door at the end of a marble corridor. Wali instructed them to wait inside. He elucidated the unwise nature of exploring their surroundings unaccompanied.

Upon entering, the students noticed myriad gigantic scrolls meticulously piled atop one another in the center of the room. Such a vast compilation of knowledge they must contain! In fascination, paces from the entrance, the students engaged in a fervent scan. Alongside the scrolls, resting on a massive wooden bureau, were brushes and inkwells of scarlet, indigo, black, and green. What a fortunate destiny have they, transcribing such knowledge onto parchment!

"If those brushes could speak," whispered Mbolaji from the entrance.

"But they do in a method all their own," said Khaleef.

They moved farther into the chamber. On each wall a fragment of the world was painted. They took care to note the details: there were oceans of deep aquamarine, with patches of forest green speckled on golden earth to represent all three continents. The room looked as if many nights had been spent pondering the pressing issues and philosophies of the civilized world, so plentiful were the scrolls and comprehensive the maps. Whilst the students imbibed the atmosphere with rapt adoration, the Baron entered.

Tunde bombarded him, "Preceptor, we have considered your words and found them irrefutable. We understand the significance of definite purpose to be paramount. Without this force, one would wander aimlessly throughout existence, manipulated much like a doll of clay. Sheer circumstance and one's own extraneous thoughts dominate he who is without purpose."

"'Tis true we have suffered loss of principle and encountered many obstacles along our path. For you, all was lost," said Mbolaji. "Your father's life, and gold as well, were taken, and your home burned to the ground. Was not your confidence ruined, your spirit dwarfed?"

"Naturally," said the Baron, "my will had been weakened. Thoughts I found, were plagued by incertitude, misgiving, and dismay. Words became increasingly hollow, causing mine actions to lack strength. In that time 'twas Nasir who pointed toward enlightenment."

* * *

"'Tis apparent the seed of fear hath taken root in thine heart. Sequester that response, lest it spread like a virus eating away at the flesh. Fearfulness is simply the mind's cognizance of weakness. Just what is it that giveth thee alarm?" scolded Nasir as we entered an eatery along the road. In the middle of the open room, robust smells emanated from brimming iron cauldrons on fires. Oh, how the spices tickled my nose. The clay floor was strewn with hay underneath the wooden tables. On each of the four walls of the establishment were archways of compressed earth that had eroded over time. The walls blended into the floor with gentle curves at their meeting points. The four archways had served as entrances for inhabitants of surrounding territories since the refectory was constructed.

As we took our seats in wait for an attendant to bring our bowls of stewed fish and vegetables, I said, "I have not the coin at my disposal to back the trueness of Father's teachings. Unenlightened men value not the knowledge of a man who showeth a want for gold."

"Will the ignorance of man make thy words untrue?" Nasir asked. "If men regard not thy words, move on. Time shall educate the unaware with painful lessons they heeded not from thee. Keep thy wisdom for the ears of understanding."

"Albeit I have studied the behaviors of powerful men, I fear that people will doubt my generalship."

To which Nasir retorted, "Sages pursue students not. Seek to ripen thine own self, not to lead men. Assurance of self emanateth from within, and from without it attracteth those who seek understanding. 'Tis similar to a piece of magnetized metal attracting its opposite. Seekers of knowledge, those who can be led, will bear witness to thy light, and those who cannot shall remain purblind."

Our meals arrived. They differed from the bowls of other patrons, for they ate flesh. As it had been an odd request, the attendant watched curiously as I feasted. Paying him no mind, I continued to list my doubts between mouthfuls. "The people are bound by ignorance to the habitual practices of ritual and tradition. I fear they will be suspicious of my doctrine as it shall contradict their deep-rooted lines of thought."

"Men can be made to move in any given direction through suggestion, or even by a manipulation of their environment. Still, thou canst not make men self-determined; they must become so themselves. Seek not to convince others of the eminence thou mightest possess, seek to convince only thyself. Let thine actions persuade when thy tongue cannot."

"I fear that those I teach might fashion a contempt for the unlearned," I complained. "For my vision to cause disdain for the unsighted would be a misfortune. Moreover, my laws might cause those easily influenced to become the marks of exploit."

Nasir held logical resolutions to mine every qualm. "Teach thy students to hold not contempt for those absent of knowledge. Omnipotence cannot be expected even of the enlightened. Knowledge is as infinite as granules of Bunzir sand. Fear not that thy power shall lead to exploitation. By empowering the willing, one not only prospereth, but ensureth survival."

"To falter during mine attempts to unfetter the minds of my brethren giveth me much fear," I contemplated. "Yet I know them to have not the understanding nor the longing to deliver themselves."

"Born solitary is each man, so too must he remove that which bindeth him to mediocrity. Prosperity rewardeth those self-assured of triumph, whilst scarcity punisheth the timid."

"The possibility that I might never be truly understood is disconcerting. The obstinate, misguided retorts of my brethren cast me further in their ignorance. Unable to relate to their state of mind, I fear to be left in solitude. The man I am destined to become beckoneth me to make haste and personify him."

Not realizing how hungry I was, I glanced down to notice my meal had since been finished. Yet I felt as though I had consumed nothing at all. Pushing the stone bowl aside, I sensed an emptiness within. Was it due to lack of food, or the mentally exhausting dilemma into which I was thrust? My body and mind were in flux.

"Assume responsibility for thine own happiness. Accept others as they come. When they do not, 'tis then thou must turn to self. Remember this and thou shalt never be alone."

The other patrons sat quietly eating, when suddenly they ogled me as I fervently exclaimed, "Why should I want such riches? Wealth is a curse. It goeth constantly lost by the hatred and incompetence of others. When I build mine empire, the king shall thieve it out of envy and greed." I must have looked a madman, having survived a fire and walking the desert till morn. Those in the room could not take their eyes from me. Some even positioned themselves the better to watch.

Nasir proclaimed serenely, "Security shan't be found in gold; history hath proven thus. Exact knowledge, experienced methods, and the ability to apply the fruit of a clear mind should serve as thy foundation. Should circumstance annihilate thine empire, let it not give thee pause. It shan't be a debilitating feat to build another if thou possessest understanding.

If thou possessest it not, then through repetition and discipline shall it be acquired."

"Father's teachings might not hold true for me. In striving I might falter, unable to recover. Then my struggle will be for naught, condemning my life to poverty. I fear being ineffective in changing this condition."

"Thou hast observed men prevail over considerable anxieties. Truth changeth not with the beholder, and man maketh not the truth. 'Tis merely a statement of the particulars as they are. He who chooseth to embrace it is wise. What would become of the babe that refused to walk for fear of falling? When a man, would he not crawl still? Fear not that thou mightest falter. As thou learned to walk, so shalt thou learn to excel. Truth is a path, not an end. Along the way, thy struggle shall bring wisdom; thy perseverance shall reap understanding." The attendant poured steaming mint tea from a small bronze kettle. Nasir paused briefly to slurp from his glass. I must have been too occupied with the disclosure of my worries to pour the tea myself. Nasir looked up, "Didst thou know thy father to be a fearful man?"

"Father experienced concern only when deliberating the perilous consequences that might result from his inaction. He could not be bothered by criticism, lest he dare accomplish nothing. To fear being affronted would mean allowing others to control his life. If he were to tolerate the festering of insecurities, he would become impotent. In allowing his mind to hold such sickness, he would surely have welcomed a much different death."

"Hast thou seen the profundity of thy words?"

I stared dumbly at Nasir, bewildered by his question.

"Art thou able to recount the tale of how Qahhar became a statesman?"

"Aye."

'Twas not soon after I consumed my fourth glass of tea that we took our leave. Once again on the desert trail into town, I spake thus, "Father was born a pauper, laboring in town as a polisher of metals. He wanted a better existence for his family than such compensation would allot. Times were hard for the peasantry, much as they are today. There was enormous competition then as well. There was a dearth of labor and merchants paid even less then. Many subsequently joined the military as a means to earn gold; Father joined as a means to advance. He conquered his fear of insolvency with that decisive act.

"Father had long since determined that his purpose would be to sit in the king's court as a noble, the highest rank bestowed upon anyone. In accordance with tradition, a mere plebe could never ascend to such a decorated post; inheritance was the only means by which nobility could be attained. Father, however, was determined to bring distinction to our name despite this decree. It consumed his every thought.

"Father etched his purpose on a scroll and hung it above the door post in his bedchamber where he could not pass without reading it. Upon rousing each morn and before retiring each night, he would quote the scroll aloud. It became his guiding thought; it possessed the necessary influence to resolve his spirit.

"When Father joined the king's regiment, he had neither a military background nor any idea how he would attain such an implausible ambition. Yet conditions known to discourage most were of little concern to Father. He eradicated the doubts that lingered in his psyche, and preferred the courage that would make the world bend to his will."

Nasir put in a word. "The Way might be filled with trials, but from each hardship one should emerge strengthened. If one is astute, a valuable lesson will reveal itself from every ordeal. An even deeper appreciation for the gifts bestowed upon thee shall be gained from all tribulations."

We came to a communal well. I paused to slake my thirst under the merciless sun, then threw mine head skyward to saturate my face with the cool liquid. Taking a moment to absorb the sheer barrenness of the desert, observing the ever-intensifying waves of heat pulsating against the horizon, we determined it best to continue, and again started toward town.

"From Father's first day as a footman in the king's army," I said to Nasir, "he thought it wise to conduct himself as a senior officer. He would inquire of himself, 'If I were king, what qualities would I look for in a general?' then respond aloud, 'One capable of leveraging collective knowledge and commanding men who are experts in specialized fields. Combat is the vocation of men at arms. Therefore, I must become well versed in military operations.' 'Twas during this form of introspection, habitually querying himself for answers, that he devised a method to solve all problems.

"With this in mind, every spare hour was spent studying historical battles, political establishments, and tactics of noteworthy leaders. All the while he analytically set preparations of his own. Father committed them to writing, ultimately amassing a compilation of scrolls.

"Father's expanding library gave him optimism," I continued. "As he began to comprehend the ways of certain leaders throughout history who had conquered in the face of opposition, his confidence escalated. He recognized how they surmounted enormous obstacles to realize prominence, even when starting from little or nothing. With each scroll a unique world opened, illuminating the methods by which their protagonists achieved success. Father's hunger amplified as he endeavored to mimic the choices of these exceptional men. This proved to be a vital assessment, capable of moving him closer to his goal. The scrolls demonstrated paths others chose to overcome their apprehensions, but 'twas Father's experiences that taught him the lessons he would need later.

"At first, Father oft shared his notions with his fellow soldiers. Unfortunately for them, they saw not his vision. Hence, in ignorance, they scorned Father, calling his words irrational delusions and outright lunacy."

"Pray, did this not discourage him?" Nasir interrupted. He broke my musing, causing me to stop and collect my bearings. So involved was I in the telling of Father's story that I was at a loss upon realizing we were halfway to our destination.

"Nay, quite the opposite. From these conversations Father conquered his phobias of criticism and rejection." I rid my forehead of more perspiration with the sodden sleeve of my robe and signaled for Nasir to join me to rest in the shade of a large sand dune. The westerly winds had picked up significantly, so I hurried to cover my nose and mouth. Nasir presented his back to me in an effort to avoid the ripping sand gales. I strained to be heard. "He chose to be wise and henceforth discussed his revelations exclusively with those who understood and would nurture his ideas. Father once told his regiment, 'Speak not to the indolent. They are quick to dismiss glorious imaginings as folly.'

"It baffled Father how men complained regarding their lack of fortune, yet sought not enlightenment from reading scrolls," I said into the wind as we reached our resting place. "Why would they sabotage themselves, engaging in negative thought and associating with weak-minded people, yet seek not the advice of a progressive voice? Father noted with regularity that the populace despised freethinkers for speaking truths. Paradoxically, he exposed that the masses embraced not reality, but that which confirmed the fabrication they endured." The whippings from the sandy winds ceased as abruptly as they had come. I cupped the sand between mine hands, watching the fine granules sift slowly through my fingers.

Nasir lay at my feet, baking under the noonday star, his hands serving as a pillow under his head. "The strong are incapable of aiding the weak unless there is a desire in them to be helped. One who is weak in spirit must develop the mettle he so admireth in one who is strong. None, save he, is able to alter his condition."

With his eyes closed as if in slumber, he continued, speaking my thoughts as if they were his own. "Lacking purpose in their own lives, these men could not possibly understand the irresistible force Qahhar sensed. He knew that just as an acorn becometh an oak, if he were both unwearied and persistent, opportunity would present itself."

"Precisely!" Amazement laced my voice. Gaining my faculties, I recommenced. "In the year of Yaseen, our king came to power. Soon after, the northern Patlaan tribe engaged us in conflict. 'Twas on a fatality-laden battlefield Father liberated himself from his fear of death. The number of casualties was incalculable. Among them lay Father's general and mentor, Bishan. He died on that campaign, training Father till his last gasp. He advised, 'The setting of the sun doth not alarm thee, nor should death; both are inevitable. Demise is but a corollary of existence. Only he who hath never lived should fear death; you—live.' With those words Bishan slipped into eternal rest.

"During this campaign, savages from the north held Father and several of his conscripts imprisoned. He endured tremendous mental strife as well as physical suffering whilst in the colony."

I stopped to catch my breath. Nasir abruptly sat up, thinking my tale had perhaps concluded. "That cannot be the end," he said.

I continued, "When Father realized the enemy could not imprison his thoughts, he was able to trounce his fear of losing autonomy. 'Twas on the seventh moon of his incarceration that Father could endure no more. He successfully led his men during a clandestine nighttime escape. Three perished in the treacherous fight. Knowing his mind was free, he knew his body was designed to follow. This epiphany spawned his escape."

"Every ordeal Qahhar was subjected to taught him valuable life lessons," Nasir responded. "To learn by his example would be most wise. Now is a perfect time to do so. Triumph over fear beginneth in the mind and is evinced through one's actions."

I replied, "Voicing the story of his life to thee in this fashion hath shed much light on many truths, I confess. Indeed, Father was a remarkable man. The situations in which he was thrust aided him in destroying his fears effectively."

Suddenly, Nasir cast his gaze elsewhere. An asp darted from its hole in the sand to catch a fleeing desert mouse. The defenseless rodent was no match for the swiftness of the snake. The glimmering black viper sprang forward to devour the creature. The serpent's jaws widened to engulf its struggling prey. Within moments the mouse was consumed wholly in the asp's gullet. "Emulate that asp in treating the phobias afflicting thy mind. Come, 'tis after midday. Let us continue our slog as we converse. We must seek shelter before we disintegrate in this heat."

We rose from the sand with some difficulty. Mine hands supported my lower back as I stretched and moaned. Finally,

I looked up plaintively at the unforgiving sun. As we trudged through the ocean of sand, the snake lazily followed as if curious of our destination.

"I fear becoming cold and calculating like the viper. That I will not feel a measure of loss when the adoration of my peers diminisheth as a result of actions I elect."

"Qahhar left the king's court with no regard of what the peasantry thought of his decision," Nasir reminded me. "In doing so, he prevailed over this fear of loss. When thou fully graspest the idea of definite purpose, thou shalt understand that it outshineth all. Moreover," Nasir admonished, "the ignorant have not the aptitude to understand thy depth of character. Consequently, why should the loss of their fickle love cause thee any concern?"

"Nasir, thy words define for me Father's actions all the more clearly. I am bewildered I did not recognize that for myself." Bored, the asp slithered lazily beneath the shade of a rock formation. Its meal was still apparent as a large swelling in its belly, slowing its pace.

"Hewers of wood and drawers of water will always find it difficult to ascertain thy meaning," Nasir resumed, "for theirs is a plane of existence with bounded policies. What is more, their rules hinder, cause lack, and obligate them; the principles they embrace are designed to instill fears that cripple them. The king wisheth to keep his people predictable so they might remain obedient. Their dogmas have no applications for thee, thus accept them not. Thy reality, be it Providence or torment, is created solely by thee."

"All notions considered equal," I continued to protest, "one could not help but fear falling ill. Sickness would either cause me to abort everything for which I have striven, or make an improper end, Nasir. Perhaps both."

"Illness would never befall one cognizant of keeping his

thoughts constructive, his physical frame fit, and sustenance nourishing. Much like the situations in which we are thrust, ill health and sickness lie defined in one's intellect. Those who fear infection are the ones, more oft than not, to be plagued. Ill-thought plans are made known through diseased bodies. A proper mindset fortifieth one's frame."

"'Tis true, yet one would still have old age," I said.

"Indeed, and with it, the experience it bringeth," Nasir responded. "One is honored for thriving through onerous times to partake in the honey of one's golden years. Wise procedures adhered to from adolescence are a simple deterrent for this unnecessary worry. Therefore, become what thou wilt. The approach thou electest may magnifyeth or crusheth anything thou mayest or mayn't wish, such as cooperation or resistance. When existence is observed as a progression of options, thou art liberated. When life goes observed as a series of obligations, thou art no more than a serf."

"Father taught me long ago, though I heeded not the lesson till presently, that there are two paradigms in which to view the world. The first existeth as choice and the other as onus. When one perceiveth an option, the mind beginneth to recognize others. In the opposite paradigm, when one's outlook is bound, the mind sealeth and induceth constant strain on the body. This thou hast reiterated to the letter and on this day I pay attention, for my life now dependeth on these words."

"Qahhar was a composed man by nature, was he not?"

"'Tis easy to be confident when all things are abundant," I answered. "Yet, how doth one increase poise from a position of utter lack?"

"Acquiring scholarship and possessing the ability to convey it produces assuredness in oneself, thereby creating a sense of preeminence over others."

I paused and rested mine hands on my thighs. My soiled, sand-whipped robes clung to me, drenched in sweat as I was from head to foot. Nasir pointedly questioned, "What is it that giveth thee doubt still?"

* * *

'Twas midday when the Baron adjourned his tale. The three pupils pleaded that he continue, but understood that other daily demands bade the Baron's attention. Before delving into his day, the Baron decreed the measures essential in attaining the invincible shield of self-confidence.

"Every night give praise to the author of nature. Recollect thy constructive notions and put thy days in review, mentally changing those occurrences not to thy liking. Ye must visualize that which ye require of the universe before manifesting it.

"Understand there shall be cycles of assurance and despair. Observe the physical frame closely when these states dominate the mind. The body must be properly utilized in order to produce desirable conditions. Duly note that confidence also cometh from one's appearance. Conduct yourselves as if always presenting the world with your vision. Rehearse your presentation before rest nightly. Do not question the viability of these precepts, accept them as exact."

Upon concluding his speech, the Baron gave his prentices free reign to roam his extensive grounds whilst contemplating the messages his account offered.

As the students strode through a recreational area designated for the children of the Baron's province, they wondered at docile animals and several contraptions that the Baron had devised purely for the children's amusement. The young knowledge seekers discussed how the Baron's father conquered his fears of rejection, futility, censure, poverty, and death.

"Qahhar proved one must build his self-confidence to survive, lest he fall victim to situations most people fear," said Tunde.

Mbolaji stopped. "Far from being an innate quality, self-confidence is acquired and developed throughout one's livelihood. We should accept that all situations are placed before us so we might reap benefit. Therefore, one must affirm that accomplishment is certain." He continued his stride with a triumphant smile.

"One should instruct the brain to supply reassuring thoughts, training the senses constantly to feel as they did during previous successes," Khaleef said. "'Twould seem logical to deposit positive attitudes into one's mind, especially before rest each night."

Wali summoned them to return for their midday meal. The scholars collected their thoughts and exited the garden. On their way inside, Tunde submitted, "These exercises have caused me to delve into mine innermost self to understand who I truly am and what my being is capable of producing. Never before have I been so thirsty for depth of character. The Baron surely hath the keenest insight of any man with whom we could align ourselves."

"A true well of knowledge, he undoubtedly is," Khaleef agreed.

THE SEEDLINGS OF EMPIRES

"Thy words of definite purpose and self-confidence have inspired me and quelled many of my fears. I am willing to endeavor, but how can I change the condition of my life when I have nothing?" I queried. I was overcome with a deep sense of hopelessness and bowed mine head.

"Nothing, sayest thou. What dost thou mean thou possessest nothing?" Nasir asked.

"I have a few supplies and two pieces of silver in my purse. Scarcely enough to eat, much less provide for anything else."

"When man initially traversed the earth, he had even less, yet was able to erect magnificent kingdoms. Considering that gold multiplieth not of its own accord, I offer that 'tis only a man lacking vision who possesseth nothing. I empathize with thy loss, but will not be party to admissions of defeat. Thy life is a chalice, newly emptied. Thou must fill it with meaning. As plainly as thou lookest into mine eyes, so hast thou come face to face with thy destiny. As with every man, 'tis in moments like these one must determine the rest of one's life."

I wanted to wallow in self-pity. So painful it was to hear such cogent words, yet I continued to listen. As his speech resonated through my mind, I remained puzzled. "I do not understand this vision of which thou speakest. Do mine eyes not behold what other men see? Do I not perceive the birds and trees just as thou dost? Do I not witness the rise and setting of the sun as would any other?"

"Indeed, thou seest the world as most men do," replied Nasir, "with thine eyes. Friend, 'tis the mind that conceiveth vision. Thou must learn to see what others do not. With prehension, thou mayest gain advantage over time and circumstance sufficient enough to shift the earth. 'Tis with intelligent foresight thou art able to make the world gravitate toward thee. Many men seek this avail. However, whilst some conceptions are right-minded, there are those deemed immoral, destructive, and self-serving."

"Wise Nasir, I have seen the devastation caused by the schemes of wicked men. That I understand, yet what maketh a man's vision transcendent?"

"I am glad thou hast finally asked such fundamental a question. Heed my words and thou shalt be saved from many defeats and unnecessary drudgery. An exemplar serveth the masses, thereby creating value."

"How can I be sure my concept will benefit others?" I queried.

"Truthfully, thou shalt not be sure it will until it is brought into existence. 'Tis at that point the masses will embrace or spurn thy design. One's conceits might seem exceptional in solitude or even in the minds of one's associates, but when introduced to the people, could face rejection. Let not thy passions for a proposed solution blind thee to the needs of thy citizenry. They will resist innovation, for change is erratic and often involveth exertion. Make them see the utility of thy method. What they sacrifice when relinquishing old ideas, they gain a hundredfold by embracing yours. Thou must enhance their lives and satisfy their wants. Diligence alone will not suffice; focus on creating value for them. As the sun's rays bring forth life, so should thy distilled thoughts.

"In addition," Nasir persisted, "thou must determine where thy goods or services are to be positioned. What market wilt thou serve, that of kings and nobles, or that of countrymen with simpler means? Thy goods or services must be priced in accordance with whom thou selectest. Thou must inspire trust in those whom thou solicitest.

"Thy planning must be precise. The world shan't resist thine offerings with proper timing. What is more, if thou art to introduce vendibles or services prematurely, thou riskest hostile criticism from the people. Still worse, others might perfect thy model. Quite the reverse, if thy timing were sluggish, thou mightest lose the advantage that cometh from being the originator of an idea."

We could see the town before us. The smell of peasant evening meals intermingled with a pungent camel stench. I had grown accustomed to both. As we drew nearer, I thought, I have no successful archetype to follow, nor the coin to change my condition. I lack a contingent of proficient individuals even to enact my wishes.

As only a soothsayer could, Nasir rebutted as if I spake aloud, "There are men thou needest seek associations with when thy wherewithal be insufficient—men with resources, knowledge, and experience. On thy quest, seek not solely men of material gain. Needed are autodidacts who are familiar with comparable services to the ones thou shalt offer."

I arrived at another realization. "Art thou implying that such visions are not self-serving? Will my conceptions not derive profit?"

"Thou shalt be rewarded in proportion to the value thou createst for others. Thus, thou must be willing to surrender thy vision to those whom thou servest. If thou art humble and listenest to the will of the people, they will define when thy tactics must change. Never lose touch with those thou servest, and in return thou shalt prosper.

"There are men from times past whose revelations have destroyed the aspirations of others. On the other hand, several of them have added benefit to civilization. If thine assertion is meant to survive, it must be of a superior mindset, better constructed, and more adaptable than those created by such luminaries and even by those they sire.

"Let not initial success blind thee with the overconfidence that naturally followeth. History dictates that one becomes the hunted because of the successful nature of one's vision. Let it be known henceforth, that when one's ideas have outlived their usefulness, one's contrivances will succumb to those that better suit present demands."

I reflected on the weight of Nasir's words so I might look for ways to fulfill those in need. Time nagged on the outskirts of my mind, as I knew the silver in my purse would soon be depleted. Upon arriving at our destined town of Daibae, I tried to identify the needs of the inhabitants scurrying about us on their way home from a hard day of labor. As we passed through the marketplace, merchants and tradesmen displayed their wares and offered various services, all with which I could not compete. I was obligated to begin a new craft, an aberrant way of thinking, but what need was left unfulfilled?

Many suns passed as I pondered what value could be created, or what necessity had gone unseen. I tried to keep myself open to every aspect of daily life, trying to find a void that begged to be filled. Of course there were discouraging moments, but I remained unyielding to the idle chatter that plagued me. Mine heart was heavy with the loss of Father and those who had died alongside him, causing my fate to press deeply into my psyche. I decided to emulate Father's way and repeat my definite purpose. The flame of my burning desire would quickly engulf any doubt that remained in my mind as it had for him.

One afternoon I happened to overhear a competition between two fellows vying for a woman's affections with ostentatious displays of masculinity. Dressed in fine regalia, 'twas apparent all three were of noble birth. Upon closer inspection, I recognized their family crests. One was significantly more endowed financially than his counterpart, as he was appareled in expensive robes and jewels. The lady raved to the pair that in her travels to faraway lands, she had come across the most delightful essenced oils. She thus proposed that if one were to acquire and present her with comparable oils as a gift, he would have proven himself worthy.

The man of more affluent birth assured the lady that with his wealth he could easily travel to any part of the world and would soon have the fragrant oils she desired. His contender, not to be outdone, elicited that he too could satisfy her whim. The lady smiled, wished them good fortune, and rode into the distance.

The two exchanged insults then parted. As the less affluent man walked, I heard him mutter nervously, "How will I win? I have not the way nor time to gain her regard!"

'Twas at this critical moment I had a pertinent revelation. 'Twas an idea that would change his condition.

"Peace be unto you. Forgive the disturbance. I could not help overhearing thy conflicted state of affairs with that fair maiden. Thou art in need of fragrant oils, yes?"

"Indeed, thou hast surmised my condition aptly."

"What do they call you?" I inquired.

"I am known as Chukah. Hast thou the means to acquire such offerings quickly and for a fair price?"

"Actually, kind sir, I do." For another, these words would have been viewed as false. But how could anyone deem them so when the heavens had provided me with such an ideal prospect?

"And what do they call thee?" he asked.

I introduced myself.

"Merchant friend, if thou couldst produce these necessary goods before the seventh sunup, I pledge to pay thee ten pieces of silver—along with my word for a larger order to follow."

Reaching for the bachelor's hand and grasping it firmly, I looked intently into his searching eyes. "I accept these terms. Ye mayest acquire them at this meeting place on the sixth sunup."

I realized that by servicing Chukah and thereby creating value for him, I would indeed be rewarded in an equitable fashion. In succeeding to fulfill such a request, I would increase my lot manifold, with the prospect of doing substantially more in trade. There were now several challenges to be addressed. How would I learn to produce oils under such time constraints? Which fragrances should I select? Would I be able to manufacture them for less than five silver pieces? Less than three, perhaps? Or was I being too ambitious?

Then I remembered Father's teachings: anything I sought knowledge of could be ascertained from consulting sapient men or their scrolls.

After asking four oil merchants for their assistance to no avail, I was forced to visit the town scrollkeeper to find materials on manufacturing fragrant oils. He provided numerous resources on the subject. As I delved into the texts, I found the process fascinating. New ideas constantly occupied my thoughts. Much of what I needed could be extracted from the local flora. It seemed most important to use high quality ingredients and be time-specific. I took the better part of the day to memorize the process and components needed until I could recite them verbatim. Afterward, with my remaining silver piece, I negotiated for the few provisions I required from the marketplace.

I laugh to think on the errors I made at first. Determined to create the best oils I could, I was careful to document my procedures, making note of successes and failures. Knowing I needed every drop of liquid, I was mindful of conservancy. By varying steps in the process, something slightly different would result. 'Twas in this manner I was able to concoct a unique fragrance that my first patron could find nowhere else. My focus left little desire to sleep or eat. The procedural log I kept became more valuable than the scrolls I originally committed to memory.

Differentiating my presentation was the next obstacle. It seemed of chief import not only to create the best oils, but also to give rise to an experience. I needed something that would win the favor of the eye immediately and inspire the trust of those who purchased my goods. Mine aim was to make the denizens buy solely from me. I wanted to create a name identifiable at once for superior quality.

The remaining days were dedicated to creating a special container for mine oils, one that would tightly seal the scent of each fragrance and keep it as fresh as the day it was made.

Attached to each bottle neck with ribbons of a lilac hue would be small hand-scribed notes to express the fragrances' origins and the care involved in their preparation. Lastly, I would stamp an insignia in the wax used to seal the bottles. I was confident the gentleman would be quite pleased.

On the sixth morn I awaited Chukah's attendance at our assigned meeting place, ready to present seven of the finest oils I could blend. The lady could have chosen a different scent each sunrise of the week, depending on her disposition.

"Kind sir, in keeping with your request, I have prepared a sampling of my finest fragrances."

I brought forth the seven vials from beneath my robes and presented them for his viewing pleasure.

"Never have I seen such detailed work for so plain an item," he said.

"Be not mistaken, my lord, these are no ordinary aromatic scents. They are the most exquisite ye shalt find in any land, far or near. The beauty of the vials merely suggests the splendor contained within. If ye art able to find a superior product, I shall return to you every piece of silver ye wilt have paid."

Visibly impressed, Chukah held each bottle to the rays of natural light, the better to see the potency of mine elixirs. I warned him not to break the seals, as he would ruin the presentation and release the initial perfumes before the lady could partake of them. He was even more awed by my description of the packages' delicateness.

"Incredible! Absolutely magnificent! I trust the bouquets held within are as beautiful as their trappings. My lady should be quite pleased. Thou hast done me a service most excellent." He pulled out an animal skin containing ten silver coins.

As he placed them in mine open palm, I thanked him. "Kind sir, 'twas a pleasure to serve you. If ye shouldst need a similar gesture of me anon . . ."

"Hold thy tongue, fragrance merchant," he said. "As thy merchandise hath captured my spirit, thou hast secured my loyalty. Never will I find such laudable quality this reasonably priced."

"That price is for you alone and should not be disclosed, for it shan't be duplicated for any other, my friend."

"I understand."

I strolled away from the transaction, head aloft and grinning as the sound of my jingling coin purse sang in mine ears. Suddenly, Nasir approached. In gratitude, I recounted my dealings since we spoke last.

Upon surveying my temperament, he surmised, "Thou art in good spirits."

"A few days prior, there was only one silver piece to my credit. With the rise and set of seven suns I have found my calling, earned nine more pieces of silver, and become proprietor of a profitable trade. Indeed, my spirits have been elevated. 'Tis not much, yet when previously I saw no morrow, now a few more seem certain," I rejoiced.

"Thou hast shown a proficiency adequate to fill a void among the people. Yet and still, hast thou created value for them?"

"Yes. No man would pay ten pieces of silver for that which he doth not value."

"Whilst thou hast created value for that man, what of others? A service to one is as far as thy vision extends? 'Tis mine opinion that thou hast much more to accomplish along that line of thought. It hath been stated earlier, with successes thine ideas shall become hunted. Those who wish to master

thine initiative will pursue thy system, for thy trade is not
unique. As thou hast emulated an established vocation, antici-
pate others to attempt the same. Therefore, be mindful of immediate rivalries."

Nasir might as well have pelted me with stones. All too
clearly the merit of his words struck me. Not bearing witness to an obvious truth when spoken would bring even
more unnecessary hardship. My surge of self-confidence from
completing the trade had now been transformed into driving
ambition.

Over the next few days I sought to improve mine existing
fragrances and invent new ones. Nonetheless, enhancing the
benefits for a larger amount of individuals continued to rack
my mind. Perhaps I should not continue in this trade. Would
it be necessary to take on another venture? Uncertainty dominated my thoughts, but I was optimistic that an insightful design would reveal itself.

A few days later, whilst procuring some supplies in the
marketplace, I encountered Chukah.

"Fragrance merchant!"

"Greetings! What an honor to see you! Might I be of service again perhaps? How did your lady respond?"

"Mouth agape, she struggled for the proper words."

"What is this? Was there a problem?"

"On the contrary, the lady adored them. She was derisive
at first when I explained the oils came not from faraway lands.
I explained that whilst 'twas easy to acquire them from afar as
she bade, doing so would only discount my love, for 'twould
have been too lengthy a journey and I had not the desire to be
away from her. Feeling mine argument was sincere, she
obliged me by viewing mine offer. She found the hand-dipped
containers intriguing, and upon breaking the first seal, the
contents transported her senses to another realm. Joy unpar-

alleled to any I had witnessed before glinted in my lady's eyes. Her skin was aglow, and her smile seemed to radiate warmth. Bringing such happiness was more than I could have asked.

"Some days later, mine opponent returned with his offering. Albeit he followed her request to the letter, in comparison to my token, she was displeased with his endowment. Neither his gifts nor the accompanying prose were embraced. With displeasure fresh on her tongue, my lady divulged that she considered her request a trial of character. In an effort to ascertain what distance her suitors would traverse, risks they would undertake, hardships they would endure for her love, she set this task before us. Upon inspecting the gift of my competitor, she reasoned he put little thought into his effort and deduced that his attempts were born of a purely physical nature. Not only did his oils pale in comparison, so too did his feigned words. If one giveth sparingly to a newfound love, surely one would sacrifice not as it matures. By way of concluding her discourse, she denied him and in turn offered me her heart."

"What a fine story, my lord! Many thanks for imparting it to me."

"Indeed, but that is not why I come to thee this day."

"Pardon?"

"Having gifted me with the key to my lady's heart and making her the envy of her fellow maidens, I bring thee another request," he announced. "I am in a position to make an offering to the king within a fortnight and wish enough fragrances to supply his court. I have but a purse of fifty and two hundred silver pieces. Albeit not much, I pray thee to find mine offer ample in consideration of the future requests thou art certain to receive as a result."

These utterances were deafening. I struggled in earnest to remain composed. The enormity of such an appeal shot fear through mine every fiber. A high-pitched ringing ensued in mine head until I could no longer hear Chukah's words, but witnessed only the movement of his lips. My palms and temples began to glisten with perspiration. Mine initial judgment screamed, "Thou darest not attempt such a feat! Thou hast not the means, supplies, nor time!" Within the span of a carefully masked deep breath, I silenced such prattle. Fear would not bar my destiny.

Exhaling, I calmly agreed, "My friend, this is excellent news! It bringeth me utmost satisfaction to know mine assistance hath brought such fortune upon you. I wholeheartedly accept your generous appeal with the following caveat. An order of this magnitude requireth a five and twenty silver piece surety, the balance of which we can happily settle within a fortnight."

"As evenhanded as always, vendor." With a simple gesture, he removed a handful of silver from his small purse, counted five and twenty coins aloud, and extended them to me.

As we parted, the once favorable sound of silver rattling in the pockets of my robes was engaging to mine ears no longer. It served only to remind me of an obligation that I was uncertain could be fulfilled. The skillful noise of a busker playing his flute masked the sound of my coins as I passed. 'Twas then I felt a pat on my collar.

"Oy, thy face conveyeth dismay. What now troubleth thee?" Nasir inquired through a toothy grin.

"I have given my word to perform a task that may be difficult to execute. The terms I have accepted are quite aggressive at this juncture. A man hath put much faith in me, with an order of grave importance to us both. Surely to disappoint him would only mean unfortunate consequences equally proportionate."

Nasir laughed jovially at my dismal commentary.

"Thou electest raillery whilst I suffer with such a dilemma?"

"Permit me to query. Why dost thou choose to entertain such pessimism? Dost thou perceive a wastrel as thy reflection is observed? The mind is promptly exhausted when permitting negativity to fester. The energy expended on such doubt may easily be applied to creative endeavors. Embrace not that which limiteth thee. How is it this man hath more assurance in thee than what thou possessest in thyself?"

"'Tis no hard effort for him to have such expectations. This man hath not my burdens."

"In matters of weighty affairs, is it not difficult to have confidence in the word of another?" Nasir rejoined. "Will not thy success or failure have more significance on his being? Thou mayest always start another trade, but this man cannot regain the esteem that will be lost as a result of thy nonperformance. Dost thou still think holding such faith in another carrieth no burden?"

"But . . ."

"Speak not of fear, for attempts to sway me with such language are in vain. The words intended for me serve only to dissuade thee, for I know otherwise. What glory will such thoughts bring? What creative abilities art thou burying?" he retorted.

I searched for an adequate response, but silence was the only reaction in my meager arsenal for such truth.

"Now then, what hast thou decided? Inaction is unacceptable."

"I shall make a way," I mustered.

"Indeed."

I began forcing myself to provide answers to all the questions in my mind. What is required of me to fulfill such a request for my faithful patron? I would have need of sufficient provisions and the aid of approximately five capable men. This would cost in excess of one hundred silver pieces! There are but thirty to my name. How might I overcome such an expenditure? The services of gold lenders were not an option, for they were beholden to the king and would surely reveal Chukah's intentions, thus ruining the surprise gift.

Pondering the quandary of creating value, I paid close attention to the way my mind generated concepts. I discovered that isolation served me well when refining mine ideas. However, I oft found the local denizens to be the most impressive stimuli for creativity. Upon studying the townspeople, I sought naturally recurring patterns that could be easily replicated, or old ideas that might be amended to create different concepts. At times, I diverted mine attention to something unrelated and would find that ideas flowed as effortlessly as water running downstream.

Considering my circumstances, I realized that success rested in mine ability to compel men to barter services or agree on delayed compensation. This would prove no easy task, for men seek immediate gratification and would likely scoff at such a precarious appeal.

When fully remunerated myself, I would reimburse merchants at a premium to their usual rate. Hopefully, these terms would be attractive enough to convince them to extend the materials necessary and start the order.

I petitioned scores of peddlers to loan me their wares, yet most stood firm on their principles. Many were unable to appreciate my posture, and therefore unwilling were they to honor my guarantee. Too often they sought the security of gold lenders to give material support to the arrangement, causing me to turn away for fear of giving up Chukah's plan.

Toward the end of the market day, when merchants were eager to make a final sale, I negotiated material costs down to fifty silver coins, ten of which were to be paid immediately, the remainder upon completion of my forthcoming transaction. Three silver pieces remained that would serve as a premium. I was left with twenty coins with which to secure labor. This could prove to be a daunting task.

Whilst collecting orange blossoms in a grove only steps from town, I came upon two men discussing their respective trades.

"My business continueth to fall on hard days. If this situation persisteth, my livelihood will be no more," confessed the first.

"Indeed, friend, 'tis a shame," replied the second. "Our prosperous days have long passed. I too have suffered dreadfully."

"In years past, my trade hath provided me abundant monetary reward. 'Tis not I for who mine heart weighs heavy, but for my neighbors. Merchants have lost either their customers or their entire trade, whilst in due course countless workmen lost their posts. They struggle for food and shelter, the bare necessities in life," expressed the first man, distraught at the plight of his community.

Finding little interest in their laments, I headed for a second time toward town. Remnants of their conversation haunted me as I walked. Their utterances directed my thoughts to our economic condition. At the time, many of the townspeople suffered from despondency, subjected to the needs and whims of the men for whom they toiled daily. I found it interesting that nearly everyone performed these exercises dutifully and without resentment. 'Twas their life's work, the reason to arise each morn. To have their regimens broken, to have their livelihoods disturbed in any fashion would, in their inexperienced eyes, culminate in times forlorn.

A chill coursed through my spine. I had been viewing my circumstances from an unfavorable perspective. Rather than ask what would compel men to extend their services with deferred compensation, perhaps the question should have been, what kind of man would be willing to do so? At last I saw a means to remove mine own hindrance, and more importantly, create value for others. These villagers would be the worthy candidates for my proposition. After all, they had needs that complemented mine own. But discretion would be vital.

This particular road on which I was traveling was laden with browbeaten individuals who had lost their posts or businesses during the fiscal plight of the Daibae Province. The first one to approach me had obviously been in his present situation for quite some time, for his slouched carriage proved he had succumbed to desolation. Attired in the robes of a pauper, the beggar had the disfigured nose of one accustomed to the drink, accompanied with two shifty eyes sunken in his weaselly head. I ignored the overwhelming stench emanating from his pores, for I knew it could not be helped. His drunkenness caused me to worry that he might not be suitable even when cleansed.

"Good man, what hath brought thee to such demise?" I asked.

"I was a noble of extensive wealth. My farmland spread toward the horizon and met the sun." His unfocused glance quickly changed direction from right to left. "Now I am like a scavenger feasting on the scraps others leave behind."

"Whatever happened to this land thou speakest of?"

He immediately stared at the ground. Then the beggar's eyes looked up to the sky as if his ancestors would shout down an appropriate response. "Our 'most exalted' king seized it all one day merely to claim the fruits of my slog to avoid drawing down his coffers," he spat sarcastically.

"Most unfortunate," I said.

I believed not a word this man spake, for the holes in his story proved him a liar. Moreover, not once did his eyes meet mine during our discourse. On this gentleman I happily passed, bestowing upon him a few coppers instead of mine offer. Though he might have done an excellent job and gone on to please me, the initial impression given was that he could not be trusted with the undertaking I was preparing to initiate. Perhaps we might cross paths again another day once his demeanor improved.

I fixed mine eyes upon a second man not far off, a lean, malnourished frame clad in tattered garb who also had a wretched air. Whilst I queried him, it seemed he was not dissimilar from his predecessor. What distinguished him were hands that revealed the marks of a recidivist, brands given by the king to habitual offenders. He would not suffice either; my merchandise and earnings would be in constant peril. In my leave-taking, I made certain my purse was fixed at my side.

In order to enliven my senses, I paused from searching for mine aides to breathe my native air deeply into my being. I needed to query as many men as I could seek out. My comfort level needed to be such that the individual I deemed appropriate held mine interests in as high regard as he would hold his own. One of mine ambitions was to offer up mine idea to others, providing the opportunity for them to embrace it as theirs. The potency of the aromatic flora I had gathered gave me a heady rush as I buried my nose into the lush bouquet. When I leveled my gaze, I noticed yet another penniless vagrant seated alongside the road.

"Sir, I beg of you, a moment, please. The sun hath risen and set thrice since I last nourished. Mightest ye spare a few coppers so that I may sup?" inquired he.

"Hast thou no means to speak of?" I probed.

"Once I had a post, but the trade was forced to close its doors. My search for another hath yielded naught. To beg for food giveth me a shameful designation. I loathe making such appeals. For what is a man unable to clothe and feed himself, or provide for his shelter? Providence seeketh to teach me humility. I shan't be unwise and ignore her lesson."

"What art thou known as?" I asked.

"Rawan," answered he. "And ye?"

I gave him my name. I was convinced this man was put in my path with a distinct purpose. Rawan's formal tone made him seem perfect for the task. His answers were practical and seemed truthful, his eyes were unfaltering, and so erect and self-assured was his posture that there was no doubt he merited an opportunity to better his condition.

"Thou seemest to be of sound mind and strong stock. Thus, I am prepared to offer thee placement in my trade, Rawan. Might such a proposition be of interest to thee?

"Wouldst ye be saying this in jest?"

"Indeed not. Thou mayest hold faith in my submission."

"I . . . I would be forever indebted to you for such a prospect," Rawan uttered. A tear sprang from his eye, seeming to cleanse the filth from his face with one distinct streak down the center of his cheek. He lunged forth and embraced me so fiercely he knocked the flowers from mine hold. We broke from one another to recollect my blossoms from the thoroughfare.

Diving into the details of the business straightaway, Rawan beseeched, "Tell me, my lord, for what undertakings will I be held accountable?"

"The making and selling of fragrant oils," I stated. "I can offer thee a wage of two silver pieces to start. 'Tis not much, I know, but I will endow thee with eight pieces more when payment has been received from my customer by the moon's next phase."

"I believe your bid to be fair for any man, particularly one who moments ago knew not how to provide for himself. My lord, I am appreciative of your offer, but regret to inform you that I lack knowledge of your trade."

"Worry not, my prentice, 'tis not a grueling process. What is more, I will teach thee the required skills."

"Oh, how fortune full! I pledge to learn quickly and do whatsoever task demanded of me with keen dedication, all to bring esteem and gold to your mark. May your generosity be looked upon with favor by the heavens."

I observed the sincerity with which this man spake, then answered, "Thou hast seen unpleasant days and suffered the pains associated with malnutrition, yet thy penury hath not been in vain. Destiny hath chosen today to smile upon thee." Out of sheer ignorance, never before would I have presupposed an individual like Rawan to be the definitive candidate to resolve my situation. This prompted mine asking, "Hast thou access to four others who might be interested in a like proposal?"

"Indeed I do, my lord! There are scores of men in the same position as I who desire nothing more than an honorable benefactor the likes of you," he affirmed with an enthusiastic nod.

"Then gather four of the most accountable and we shall commence posthaste. We will meet at my temporary workshop, the shed of the old linen weaver, on the northern edge of town."

"With pleasure, my lord!"

A man of his word, Rawan appeared with four men just after the noonday meal. At first glance they resembled one another, with sooty faces and threadbare garb. They no doubt had similar stories of misfortune. However, upon further inspection it was apparent their ragged clothing bore no reflection on their character. Excitement and zeal twinkled in each of their eyes, making their desire quite obvious.

Motioning Rawan aside to speak in confidence, I commented, "Thou hast fulfilled mine initial request in a timely fashion, friend. This pleaseth me to no end."

One of the four was barefoot as he stepped forward. "My lord, allow me to introduce myself as Jalaal. On behalf of the rest, we appreciate the occasion not only to earn silver, but also to master a craft. Ye hast found utility where none else foresaw such potential. We had even lost our own dignity. Because ye allowed us to feel whole, as men should, we are forever in your debt."

Hands clasped in gratitude, the men nodded earnestly.

"'Tis only appropriate to repay kind words with those of mine own," I said. "Honored am I to stand before men like you. Today is a glorious day. Before, we lacked the ability to progress unaided. Misfortune had seized our spirit, sense of meaning and purpose. An opening is before us. The opportunity of which I speak is the ability to reclaim that which was taken from us. Seek not to labor in pursuit of gold, but of excellence. Not to compete, but to innovate. Proceed not from haughtiness, but from respect for your brethren. Let not success bring you contentment, nor failure bring you sorrow.

"Place the needs of your patrons before your own interests. The market may determine the rate of your goods, but never your sense of worth. Surely, there will be times when life will see fit to teach us lessons of failure and disappointment. We shall have our time. If not this day, then the subsequent one. If not this trade, another. Be unmoved by circumstance, but remain steadfast to these principles. Before we may become masters of industry, we must gain full command of self. 'Tis with these words your vision should be clear and footing certain. By way of finishing, I submit to you a promise. Offer the world unreserved value and ye shall not be forsaken, but rather compensated by Fortune in direct proportion."

Awestruck by mine heartfelt words, Jalaal shook himself aright, cleared his throat, and spake for the lot once more. "Ye hast inspired us to make use of our circumstances. We are beholden to your mission."

"Then I am of the belief that we are prepared. Let us make ready."

The sun rose and set twice more as I instructed the men in my method for making oils. They worked diligently and caught on quickly. I taught them the techniques that had brought successes as well as failures, in the hopes that they not repeat the latter. By passing on knowledge that was critical to the trade, each man was given a sense of entitlement over the process. I declared that I expected not only excellence, but also innovation. They were taught not only to question, but to improve.

Giving a sense of ownership was vital in communicating that their efforts were appreciated. If one had an idea, rather than judge it, he was challenged to prove his theory. His proposed model would have to demonstrate the practicality of his construct and the market would hence certify its viability. The men often had spontaneous ideas during nighttime hours. Such passion brought not the desire for rest. They saw the production of oil not as the manufacturing of a good, but as personal growth. Their passion was captured in every bottle. Once comfortable with the procedure, each developed several unique fragrances. Their focus worked to create fifty and one hundred oils for my line, whilst mine efforts yielded another five and twenty.

We were prepared to go before Chukah on time as promised. I summoned him by way of messenger and met him accordingly in the melon fields.

"Greetings, Merchant! How art thou?" questioned he with a wide smile.

"Quite well, and you, kind sir?" I asked.

"Blessed, friend, with the good fortune to walk land another day. I am in excellent health and revel in the love of a woman who understands me fully."

"Wonderful to hear how prosperity continues to smile upon you."

"Thank thee, and may it do unto thee in a likewise fashion. Pray tell, hast thou an order for me?"

I presented mine associates, who aided me as I displayed their concoctions, each bearing my seal.

"This is remarkable. Once again thou hast done superbly. I have come to expect nothing less," commented the patrician.

"There is but one thing more. Because ye art such a loyal customer, I have elected to create for you exclusive oils. No other shall have these, ever. They belong to you. If ye findest it in your favor, present one as an offering to your king and the other to your lady."

"This is a wonderful surprise. I am very grateful, many thanks. As promised, here is the balance of thy payment, five and twenty plus two hundred pieces of silver. I shall be certain to relay the news of mine offering to thee."

With Chukah's money, I repaid my forty silver piece debt, plus a premium of three, to the merchant who sold me supplies. Then I sought out my men to remunerate them.

"My noble has purchased the goods, and as promised, I owe each of you eight pieces of silver. I wish to dispense two additional pieces each in a show of gratitude. Rawan, please distribute these fifty coins amongst yourselves."

Rawan divided up the silver betwixt the craftsmen.

"Ye have all shown innovation, competence, and unity. Such values are to be rewarded. They bring success, improve one's character, and create the finest merchandise for our patrons. In less than a fortnight ye have seen twelve pieces of silver. I ask that each of you set two aside in order to begin investing in fortunes of your own."

"Ye hast been more than generous and offered us means of acquiring food and shelter. How can we accept a payment we have yet to earn?" queried Jalaal.

"Believe in your hearts that ye deserve this reward, for had I not offered you a perquisite, surely Life would have done so. An admirable feat, ye have improved yourselves, and are now able to advance your circumstances. Ye have strengthened my trade so that it may bring laudation and yield. To share it with you hath been mine own blessing. Understand, good men are more important than gold. Like the seasons, capital is fleeting, but honorable men weather the storms. Ye have not dissatisfied me, therefore, I shall not fall short. Remarkable ye are; from you many successes are expected. Whatever ye might need to achieve prominence, ye shall have it provided."

Our bond became unbreakable as the group understood their significance. From that day, I had their loyalty. I became known as a just leader who esteemed my workmen. Expectations were clearly defined and they were given the freedom to create.

Some time later, Chukah returned with a report of his offering.

"Fragrance Merchant, I have wonderful news! My present was an enormous success! Thy gift hath brought our names immense praise! News of thy mark quickly spreadeth to neighboring kingdoms. Bombarded was I with questions of thy trade, and of course I withheld nothing. I would not be the least surprised to know thy trade was overwhelmed with orders as early as the morrow. The king was especially pleased, which in turn caused my lady to be overjoyed. I am drunk with admiration. Thy skill is unparalleled."

"I bid you thanks, my friend. Veneration from a highly respected noble is the most effective form of public notice I can surmise."

"'Tis a puzzlement how a youthful man such as thyself could possess so much wisdom."

"Ye meanest to flatter me, yet I may not accept such credit. The only wisdom I possess cometh from observing and respecting the deeds of the truly wise. Then and only then do I act accordingly."

"Perhaps then, I spoke out of turn."

"What dost ye mean?" I inquired.

"That is not wisdom, that is genius. Simple as thy declarations may seem to thee, such innate sagacity is not common, especially amongst those who presume themselves to be learned."

"I am humbled. 'Tis perhaps true."

"Without question, 'tis truth," Chukah said. "I cannot recall seeing even a noble as young as thee possessing such understanding of life and building a profitable trade of his own. What is it that motivates thee? Gold? Acclaim? Imperium?"

I answered, "In all honesty, it is none of those. Mine aim is to serve others. I was once told that he who solely desireth money and fame eventually faltereth, finding no glory when all is said and done. However, he who createth value for others will have his own interests provided for proportionately."

"Thou obviously hast taken in the counsel of the wisest advisors."

"'Tis acknowledged that the accomplishments of men who seek counsel in those wiser than themselves shall be limitless," I said.

With a reassuring pat on my shoulder, Chukah declared, "And so shall it be for thee. Mine only wish is that my nephew had ambition the likes of yours. There is a man who hath yet to mature. Instead, he wasteth time indulging in trivial pursuits and destructive pleasures. Perhaps thou mightest talk to him one day, pass along some wisdom that may help him find a higher meaning in life?"

"I would consider it an honor."

After parting with Chukah, I saw it fit to visit the public bath before the evening meal. Whilst refining myself, I happened upon Nasir once more as he too was performing his daily cleanse. We exchanged a few thoughts as we bathed among other families.

"Considering this successful trade, I wish to raise prices."

"Hmmm . . . would a higher price provide a value greater or lesser for thy patrons?" tested Nasir before disappearing into the water below.

"I have come to recognize that value goeth perceived in the beholder's eye," I reasoned when he resurfaced. "The majority of my potential consumers in this, as well as the neighboring towns, are nobility. They undoubtedly wish to differentiate themselves from each other and those they rule. They also wish for the best, so a higher rate will provide few objections. I shall veil my charge with exclusivity and lure them with the highest quality standards. If I aim to attract commoners, I will have to reduce prices and might alienate my current patrons."

"I pass no judgment on the man who serveth kings and

nobles over plebeians, yet art thou certain both markets are mutually exclusive? Art thou not capable of servicing them equally?"

"That matter would require a far more comprehensive ponderment," I responded.

Nasir said, "A review of the value concept may provide an adequate answer."

I left the bath considering Nasir's comments. My focus remained on enhancing the well-being of the largest number of people I could. Always seeking inspiration, I decided to take a longer, more scenic route. On my way to nourish at a local eatery, I reflected in the hope an idea would reveal itself.

I passed the clothing merchants in the marketplace and observed the difference between fabrics they marketed toward affluent persons and toward those with lesser means. Of particular interest was a merchant serving both groups at the same stand. The epiphany suddenly struck me.

Two classes of goods could be devised, one to target nobility and the other aimed at the townspeople. Each would bear different seals. This way, the townspeople could feel they too were able to experience quality at a fair price, whilst the exclusive collection would allow the aristocracy to feel their needs were being satisfied. A premium rate would be charged for exclusive oils. Then for the townspeople, the same quality currently being fashioned could still be produced. This would serve both markets and spare little for future competitors.

Ambition energized my thoughts and gave rise to an immediate need for action. Without further ado, I beckoned my prentices to submit my model.

"Brothers, a moment of illumination hath stricken me," I exclaimed.

"What is this light? Tell us, please," insisted Rawan.

"I have been deliberating the idea of value. I inquired of myself, 'How might we grow our list of patrons without alienating our loyal buyers?' There were many factors to mull over. Ultimately, the best option seems to be designating two distinct lines, both comprised of the highest-quality product. One shall carry an elevated price and be formulated exclusively; the other shall be produced in mass quantities for a modest charge and then allocated to those of slighter funds. This stratagem should offer the most effective means of creating value for the highest number of patrons. We shall make the world believers in our vision."

We proceeded to manufacture both lines that very day. Chukah's forecast was accurate, as orders from the king's court flooded in. No amount of preparation could have readied us for the volume of interest that ensued. I highlighted our exclusive collection. As expected, kings and patricians favored the private label, and the lower classes longed to sample it for themselves. The community quickly realized the superior quality of our modestly priced scents and relished in the ability to purchase them. Where once before the townspeople could never dream of partaking in the daily luxuries of the aristocracy, I had made available the key to their want.

Before long, my men and I had a newfound wealth from the prospering trade. News of mine identifying mark traveled quickly and had become praised throughout distant lands.

Several moons had passed. As fortune would have it, I encountered Nasir browsing for a brooch in an elite garment house in the territory. I decided to join him in his perusal.

"Qahhar would be elated to know thou hast prospered so," commented Nasir.

"Indeed, my trade hath done quite well."

"That it hath, but I doubt that is what he would find most agreeable."

"No?"

"Thou hast not yielded to any hindrances, not even thine own reservations. Upon discovering how to look within self, where thou once saw nothing, thou now witnessest the infinite power of creation. In proving that these lessons have been learned, thy father would be filled with pride. Yet, what of thy men? What reward shalt thou bestow upon them?"

"Have I not rewarded them amply?"

"Certainly. Nonetheless, can sheer monetary gain compareth to the esteem one feeleth when executing one's own vision? Wealth alone granteth little contentment," Nasir said with his signature gruffness. "By limiting thy men to pecuniary compensation, thou hast limited their initiative and denied them true happiness. Thou must help empower them to create."

I left the clothier with thoughts of how to further enable my workmen. After some deliberation, I determined I would offer a partnership to them. This ought to give them an even stronger sense of entitlement. They could branch out to faraway lands, establish shops of their own, and expand the initiative even further.

The following eve, I called everyone together to banquet at a popular refectory. We took refuge at a large table in an empty corner where I was mindful to keep my voice under strict control as I spake.

"Good men, ye have provided me with invaluable services for which I am extremely grateful. To show my gratitude, I offer you individual partnerships and locations. Each of you should extend to other territories where ye would reside and be master craftsmen. Conduct your trade just as we have done so here. Hire good men with sound ideas who seek advancement, regardless of birth or circumstance. Ye shall be held responsible for everyday activities, creating new ideas and bringing your visions to light. Do ye accept these terms?"

Fully absorbing the meaning of my declaration, they looked at one another in disbelief that such fortune could happen upon them once more.

"My lord, ye hast compensated us more than fairly and provided unimaginable liberties. Such a gift cometh subsequent only to the hope given us when before we had none to speak of. 'Twould be an honor to represent your mark," said Rawan.

"Then it is done! We shall hold a celebration and invite our patrons to announce the expansion."

We merrily ate, drank, and shared our memories that evening. We planned for the festivities to take place on the next lunar phase. Our patrons came from everywhere the eye could see. The revels served as excellent public notice for all who were unaware of our mark. In total, the occasion proved to be a success.

Not long after, the men were ready to establish new exchanges elsewhere. They packed up the belongings they acquired whilst under mine employ and left for their journeys. The problems they encountered along the way were only stepping-stones to prominence. In time, they found comparable success to the first model I launched and were endowed with many days of prosperity. The principle of creating value for others to reap subsequent benefits had been made clear to me.

* * *

"Pupils, ye are intelligent men," the Baron remarked. "Therefore ye are obligated to create ideas that direct those less practiced, rather than bend your backs laboring under their employ."

He led his students into the assembly hall of the Grand Fiduciary Council just off the riverbank on the outskirts of the province. The council was a consortium of experienced benefactors who had previously joined forces with the Baron to facilitate ventures from those whose models had withstood a gauntlet of interrogation. These men were from all walks of life; they had developed existing trades or started ones of their own in order to better society. They labored not solely for remuneration, but also for the opportunity to present their ideas before the deliberative body. It created value for them in the form of purpose. The students looked about with mounting interest. The Baron noted their curiosity.

"Great ideas come from the most unforeseen sources. One should be cognizant of seeds that have the ability to grow into empires. These seeds come in myriad forms from men in positions of both stature and ignobility. Within each man lieth a seed of this ilk that either remaineth dormant without a proper impetus, or germinateth into a flower that spreadeth its pollen to others."

"The first men ye tookest under your employ gave the impression of being eager to develop their status, much like those we observe here in this consortium," Tunde said. "Yet, before making your association, the initial hires spoken of in your tale appeared unable to improve themselves. Were they not then bound?"

"Bound to mediocrity, of course. Yet when a man ceaseth to gripe and discerneth the integrity buried within that will advance his lifestyle, only then is he truly an illimitable being. Understand, till one's goal and lateral thinking work together, no form of success can exist."

Mbolaji paced then brusquely turned back toward the group. "Oh, how imprudent I have been! Seeking wealth unaccompanied, returning from my daily pursuits slight, or what is worse, empty-handed. Not until this moment have I truly recognized it necessary to invalidate my current philosophy. 'Tis a sound approach to supply individuals with whatsoever they need to create the farthest-reaching benefit and improve the lot of each involved."

The Baron studied this pupil, then retorted, "Despite how capable one is, one still cannot achieve success alone. One hath a duty to grow one's enterprise and create value for others. Therefore one is cheating himself, his vision, even the world, when attempting success alone. One can only do so much without aid."

Khaleef elected silence as all eyes turned toward him. The Baron felt his hesitation and smiled. "Ofttimes he who observeth whilst others exchange is left with the best position of all. Enough today—allow me time to converse with my fiduciaries."

With that, the Baron directed Wali to escort the trio back to the estate where, into the night, they scribbled away on their tablets, determined to record the lessons taught them.

WITHIN THE SPAN OF SEVEN BREATHS

One balmy day, my loyal patron, Chukah, approached me. He was wearing an expression of perplexity on his brow whilst browsing the marketplace.

"Fragrance merchant, how art thou this morn?" he asked.

"Of high spirits, sir, many thanks for the inquiry. And you?"

"In all honesty, friend, I am quite troubled."

"Perhaps I may be of service in some way . . ."

"I spake of my nephew, Hassid, on a previous occasion. He is an idler, plagued with indecision and in need of direction. His days go unstructured; his actions are halfhearted."

"Wouldst ye like for me to have a few words with him?"

"Actually, I had hoped thou wouldst agree to oblige me a spot further."

"How dost ye mean?" I questioned whilst eyeing several sticks of wax for my seals.

"I was thinking perhaps my nephew could find a post in one of thy branches in order that thou mightest provide him with guidance."

I said, "A post for him certainly might be arranged, but as for this guidance of which ye speakest, I, sir, am no sage."

"Thou art far too modest, Merchant," Chukah declared. "Thy wisdom is certain to be recorded before long. This gesture, if granted, shan't go unreciprocated."

"I could not refuse the man who made much of my success possible. 'Twould be an honor. Bring him before me so we may begin training upon the morrow."

"Indeed," Chukah agreed. "Thank thee so very much. I am forever in thy debt for this indulgence."

The following morn, Chukah and his nephew made their way toward my tiny shed behind the old linen weaver. It was used as an inventory stall, as I only made oils when our most esteemed buyers should personally request it.

The young man accompanying Chukah showed his displeasure by halting their advancement to bicker. I observed them from a seat behind my work desk.

"I am a noble!" he exclaimed aloud. "This is no place for a man of distinction! What hast thou brought me to witness, Uncle?"

"Hast thou no respect for knowledge and wisdom?" Chukah upbraided, irate at such an outburst. "Dost thou know the means to maintaining a lucrative trade?!"

"Our family owneth vast amounts of land that generate profitable yields. I require not the knowledge of oil manufacture, nor the want to strain for anything."

"Thy father hath placed thee in my charge, for he wisheth thee not to squander his holdings. Thou possessest little knowledge as to how the yields of which thou speakest are even brought to harvest. When the time cometh to lead and show thine offspring the path to prosperity, thou wouldst not be capable of doing so. If thou electest not to become a master tradesman, how might thou increasest thy purse, let alone continue in thy father's wake?"

"Might I interject?" I asked from my window.

"Please do," grumbled the weary uncle.

"Young Noble, if a merchant wished to have a loan of five hundred silver pieces against his goods, what rate wouldst ye charge?" The lad gave no indication of responding, so I continued, "If a messenger of your king were to offer fifty and eight hundred gold coins for your father's land on the western riverbank, what would your offsetting bid entail?"

"There are scholars who answer these questions for less than twenty silver pieces," the young man spat.

"Wouldst ye truly wager the fortune of your father and your own future on a man whose stipend is a mere twenty pieces of silver?" I pressed.

"Trade, in and of itself, is an industry built on trust," Chukah's nephew replied. "Couldst thou say with sound mind that thou gamblest not thine income on the knowledge of other men everyday?"

I answered him with ease. "Evidently the difference is unclear to you. Based on a system of checks and balances, I have trained men in methods that I have established. There is no man in mine employ who would claim to know more about my trade than I."

"Thou art but a slave—" quarreled the boy.

"How darest thou insult mine ally?" scolded his uncle as he struck the youth on the back of his head.

"Please, friend, allow him to speak freely. The words of another shall never cause me to be affronted. They are to be heeded as accurate or dismissed as absurd. Please, resume," I said.

After hearing my request, the young noble softened. "Forgive mine insolence, Merchant, for mine uncle is correct. My careless tongue doth escape me. I desire not to offend thee, for thou hast done me no harm. 'Tis merely mine opinion that time is of principal value. I regard it as more precious than gold. I have become a man of means by way of inheritance. My forefathers have acquired wealth so that I might benefit from it without labor of mine own. I wish not to be a slave to a trade, nor to rudimentary knowledge."

"'Tis true, a man might benefit without travail, but never without actual thought," I added. "There are men who will teach that labor purifieth the soul; they omit that 'tis not physical, but mental labor of which they speak. Just as a warrior might say that victory can be achieved without battle, wealth can also be attained without physical labor."

"What fortunes hast thou secured of thine own volition that would permit thee to claim such insight?" questioned Chukah of his nephew. "What victories hast thou tallied to profess such hubris? Who art thou to debate the experienced and learned?"

"Admittedly, I have earned nothing independent of Father's holdings. I have accomplished relatively little without his aid or influence. I do possess some knowledge, 'tis experience I lack. But are momentous ideas not brought about from inner-directed thought? The exercise of such license should not go scorned in this fashion," the young man defended.

"Revolutionary ideas merit respect," I said. "However, the men who spawned these ideas snatched them from the heavens. They do not own their gift. Truly noble points of view belong to the general public and must be utilized to their advantage. When clever men prosper, 'tis only through the gifts they used to benefit others. Your very life is not your own. Instead, ye art relegated as a mere instrument of service," I affirmed.

"I beg to differ. I do not exist for another. This life is mine own," the inexperienced nephew persisted.

"Ye art but one. The delights ye pursuest anywhere other than serving your brethren shall be short-lived. Canst ye not see, 'tis far more rewarding for all involved to bring fulfillment to the masses? Dost ye think it a coincidence that ye were born as ye art? Friend, ye too have a mission to do magnificent work. This is why ye hast been granted use of diligent men and vast wealth. Your elders all have honor and respect associated with their marks, 'tis now your turn. Ye art charged with finding your vision and changing lives for the better."

"Why should it be my duty to develop persons unfamiliar?"

"Ought it not, Hassid?" asked his uncle.

"The condition of your brother will inevitably become yours," I added to Chukah's argument. "Is it not wiser then, to pass on good fortune, rather than be selfish with the privilege it hath afforded you? Such a disposition will surely bring solitude."

"Again, why must I shoulder the world's burdens?"

"Because ye hast been blessed with a gift, means that extend beyond your immediate needs," I responded. What an indomitable young man. His energies needed a strong mind to redirect him on the correct path; his uncle had expressed the truth when he came to me for aid.

"But I cannot help those men," Hassid insisted.

"At present, perhaps not. If it is a righteous path ye seekest, then ye shalt find your way."

"Now 'tis immoral to have desires for oneself?" he asked, incredulous.

"Why wouldst ye not aspire for your brethren that which ye seekest to attain?" I posed. "Serving others leadeth to realizing one's meaning in life."

Hassid had yet to be convinced. "Merchant, how is it that thou mayest define purpose for me?"

"Ye art too presumptuous, 'tis not my definition. Rather, what dost ye think bringeth substance to one's existence if not service to others? Ye mayest enjoy wealth, yet in how much libation might ye partake? In how many chariots shalt ye be carried? When shall your gluttony at last be fulfilled? I shall no longer attempt to convince you. Further, I shall not pass judgment upon you, as I may only evaluate mine actions. I propose only a way. If it is right for you, ye wilt elect it."

"Couldst thou be so callous as to see thy brother struggle and hold not compassion?" asked Chukah. "I challenge thee to find a man of benevolence, upon whom the heavens have shined, that hath not been of service to others."

"Thou art assuming the people want mine aid."

"Indeed, just as we are presuming ye might benefit from this intervention," I told Hassid. "Ye shouldst not forsake your brethren an opportunity because they might not understand the rewards of your offer. Even if ye dost not attempt to sway them, the prudent will seek you for guidance. If one is sincere, deny him not. The ways of the world are such that what ye givest of yourself shall return to you magnified. Be vigilant, for giving coin to the improvident will result in it leaving their hands in accordance with their lack of knowledge. Share your understanding so they might build their fortunes, and ye shalt find yours will increase manyfold."

"The merchant speaks truth, Hassid. What higher form of knowledge shalt thou acquire with thy methods? Let not thy stubbornness as it pertains to time's value become thy bondage. Reflect on the costs associated with what thou mightest lose or gain with such decisions. To which side doth thy measure lean?" queried Chukah.

Hassid turned to his uncle. "Thine urgings have been noted. If I am to labor and gain not an equivalent recompense, I expect no further wrangling from thee."

"Unapprised one, 'tis only because the sweat of labor hath never touched thy brow that thou dost not realize that one may never toil without a reward equal or surpassing in effort."

The youth grumbled, "How shall I begin?"

I responded, "Ye shalt travel to all of my stations. Study them a fortnight each until ye finally understandest the subtle differences between their procedures and marketplaces. Speak with townspersons to uncover their dislikes about our wares. Think up a list of curative actions and prepare a scroll. Bring it before me on the fourth new moon. Your journey will be laborious, but I am confident in your ability to successfully carry out the task." I tossed him a purse of sufficient weight. "This should cover your expenses."

"As I have given my word, I shall deliver my report upon completion of this grueling assignment. Allow me to make preparations and leave for my first destination upon the sun's rise," muttered the defeated Hassid. He turned away with his head bowed in humility.

"I did not expect thee to assign him such a formidable undertaking," said Chukah. "I thought a sinecure would suffice."

"I hope ye art not displeased?" I queried.

"On the contrary. 'Twas unexpected is all."

"To assign him a small post would have communicated an ineffective message. By assigning him a mission of larger significance, I hope to communicate that from him I expect merit. The prentices that comprise my workforce are all recipients of similar treatment. This lesson is not about a wage, 'tis about ownership, advancing a vision, and eventually laying claim of one's own trade."

"Again thou impressest me with thy shrewdness. Thine actions are insightful, daring. I ought to have expected such from a man of self-possession," commented Chukah.

"Although I am appreciative of such words, mine actions are unworthy of this esteem. I have made but a simple gesture that might afford him the opportunity to reveal his true self."

"Thine humility is admirable, but this noble quality doth little to veil thine acts of generosity. I have encountered few men who exhibit thy soundness of mind. In due course, thy destiny will call to thee."

I graciously smiled at his compliment as we made our departing remarks.

A season had come and gone, and it was soon time for Hassid to return. As yet, I had neither seen nor heard word from him since his leave-taking. Seventy suns had I seen, and still the young man had not appeared. When finally my concern could bear no more, I sent word to my brethren in trade, inquiring of his whereabouts. On the rise of the half-moon, the young man returned.

A look of exhaustion and dismay accompanied him; thus, I greeted Hassid with food and drink. Before he could offer any explanation, I granted him three day's rest to collect himself and prepare his report.

Upon the second day, Hassid came before me, visibly troubled.

"What burdens you?" I queried.

"I have failed thee, Merchant."

"Come now. How could this be?"

"My scroll remaineth unmarked. I secured not the information thou required and squandered mine allowance on vices," he confessed.

I could only shake mine head, amused at the young man's folly.

"What dost thou find so humorous?" Hassid asked, insulted by my response to his troubles.

"Your actions, of course," I answered. "Tell me then, didst ye learn nothing in your travels? Frittering your stipend must have yielded you some wisdom in hindsight."

"Not in the ways of trade, no."

"The gold that once occupied your purse now belongs to another. Didst ye not learn a lesson from the exchange?" I encouraged. "What words of blandishment did your tempter speak that caused you to stray from your journey? Further, what void within yourself made you unable to resist his ploy? Every transaction revealeth something about the patron and merchant. An astute customer learneth to distinguish his needs from desires, along with the vending techniques of the merchant. A wise tradesman taketh the principles he learned when a patron and applieth them accordingly."

My words seemed to shudder his very being, rendering him speechless. Gathering himself, Hassid started, "I thought my decisions were of mine own will, but in effect, they were the manipulations of others."

"Ah, arrive not at such a hasty conclusion. In every meeting of commerce, someone is sold. Either the merchant selleth a patron on his wares, or the patron selleth the merchant on his disinterest. Be careful not to place total responsibility on another when your actions are at fault. Didst ye lack the discipline to refuse?"

"Indeed I possess such restraint and shall offer no more excuses. Please, if permitted another chance, I will prove capable of exercising composure," he begged.

"I freely give but one opportunity, all others must be earned."

"But, Merchant—" Hassid interrupted.

"If I were to give you another chance undeserved, I would only be delaying the lesson your missteps endeavor to teach you. If ye art to stay under my charge, such an opportunity shall be merited from the lower ranks."

"I vow to bring no further shame to thy mark. I shall serve thee with the honor thou deservest."

After pondering the matter, I said, "If ye art sincere, ye shalt have one chance at redemption. The path is not a smooth one, nor is it effortless. Your fortitude will surely be tested at points. Place not all your faith in a guide, as total reliance in another will fail you."

"I understand."

"As your knowledge must grow to accomplish anything, your instruction shall begin anew. Ye shalt study scrolls to gain an understanding of how to improve my trade. Ye must be able to recite their contents verbatim. My workforce and I shall be readily available for your inquiries regarding these matters.

"Be cautioned of the three mentalities of those who read scrolls," I continued. One faction hath realized new societal paradigms and seeth fine details that may be varied upon and improved. This hath allowed them to eclipse antiquated ways of thought. Another group seeth only the theme as presented, and is far too rigid to flesh out deeper insights. In fine, a third mindset, which is utterly lost, seeth merely ink on papyrus."

Hassid nodded.

"Ye hast one moon to complete this study."

When the assigned duration passed, Hassid returned.

"Merchant, shall I recite for thee the contents and procedures to create all fragrant oils?"

"Ye mayest now hold the knowledge of the scrolls. However, what innovative understanding hast ye gained from them?" I asked.

"Additional insight hath eluded me."

"Then ye shalt assist in the gathering of materials for yet another moon. Your objective is to improve my trade. Let not the physical nature of your post deaden your mind. Ye art required to think at all times and in all roles as would a master tradesman. We shall meet again upon the end of the scheduled period."

As soon as the moon raised full once more, my charge reemerged with his account.

"Young man, what new ideas hast ye divined?"

"I have met a local carpenter who can create a tool for expressing thine oils with speed. Production would occur at twice the current pace."

Excited by his report, I prodded, "What is the quality of such a yield?"

"The output compareth not to thine exclusive oils, but 'tis of equal measure to the line designated toward those of slighter means," Hassid said whilst offering me a sample of several fragrances.

Appraising the concoctions in each vial, I said, "Ye hast made a valiant effort, but regrettably, I cannot say they are of comparable quality. I hesitate in giving such goods my mark. Perhaps we should continue with our current methods."

"Mightest thou affirm now? Such a technique will surely be the standard one day."

"In my craft, I have had many failed attempts with various methods. The cost of perfecting his system seemeth far too rich. I shall give it further consideration, but as yet, I am undecided."

Upon my lack of enthusiasm toward his proposal, Hassid's face, once beaming with excitement, had turned glum.

"Fret not, your diligence hath merited the occasion to redeem your previous transgressions. Ye wilt shadow my movements for an annum. Within that time, ye shalt gain the comprehension of every aspect regarding my trade. This includeth governing men and operations, as well as bartering with merchants and securing loans from usurers. As such, ye shalt have the power to negotiate on behalf of my mark. Let not privilege cloud your judgment, for only honor and respect truly strengthen bonds. Be forewarned, mistakes made in generalship of the trade impinge not only on yourself, but also upon your purchasers and the livelihood of your staff. The profits recorded in the scrolls are but a past measure of the satisfaction of one's patrons and workforce; they hold only momentary glory. If ye shalt fail either, your livelihood will wither. Ye must conduct yourself honorably; disgraceful deeds reap naught."

"I understand," Hassid replied.

Autumn turned to wintry weather, then an invigorating spring to a clement summer. I instructed Hassid in every detail of trade. I inculcated mine affirmations to force out his inexperience. He often made mistakes not even one untrained would make; I began to question his resolve. He showed signs of indifference at times. When sent on missions, he failed to accomplish them. Mistakes were unacceptable, for the market is unforgiving. I queried why he would not try various approaches. He offered excuses, and I told him they served as a poor shield. Was I incorrect in believing so profoundly that such a capable man could surmount these obstacles?

Ultimately, he began to understand that triumph was the only tolerable outcome. I disciplined him to be decisive. 'Twas important for Hassid to learn anticipatory measures. If problems occurred, hesitation would be costly.

"Hassid, I have duties to attend to in Hyrangea on the southern coast. Until I return, the trade and the administration of all its branches will be in your charge."

"Why not Rawan or Jalaal? They are far more experienced than I," he implored with a quivering voice.

I smiled. "Hast ye no desire for glory? Sure, Rawan and Jalaal have more experience, as do mine other three master craftsmen. But today is yours; be as the sun. Or wouldst ye rather gravitate and reflect as the moon?"

"I fear not the thought of filling thy position."

"That is what I expect to hear from a man willing to carry such a post," I said. "Men of abundant resources do not fear command. They intend for higher profits than accrued twelve moons prior. Your foremost concern should be to preserve your wealth before seeking its furtherance," I tutored. "Therefore, be not reckless in pursuit of your objective."

At dawn, I gathered scrolls in a carrier and saddled my mount. I was confident the right decisions had been made.

I arrived several seasons later upon receiving word to return posthaste. There were troubles with a number of my shops. Traveling through town, I was inundated with complaints. Merchants were disgruntled at mine increasingly tardy payments, my men were shorted their recompense, and patrons received orders in error. Debt compounded exponentially whilst profits had dissipated. There was even a fire at my post in the west.

I sent for Hassid.

"What hast ye done?"

"We were beset by competition. The carpenter—"

"I have not the time to deal with such issues. I must meet your uncle and the king to discuss a potentially lucrative venture. Upon my return, these matters will be summarily dealt with."

"Fragrance Merchant, thou must listen."

"My time is wasted on such ponderments. At present my thoughts are engaged with more significant priorities; I shall rectify your concerns anon."

Once again I ventured out of the territory, leaving Hassid to tend to the matters as best he could. Upon mine homecoming, no more than eight sunrises from the last we spake, my flourishing business had become insolvent. The men had not been paid and my brothers had incurred debts. Hassid's ineptitude had swelled into a fine mess. Again I sent for him.

"Ye had not the time to cause this much worry. Where didst ye falter?"

It was then that a gentleman approached on horseback. A half-dozen hired soldiers accompanied him. "Fragrance Merchant, we come to seize thy property and settle thy sums unpaid."

"Seize! Who art thou?"

"I collect for several of thine usurers. Thou hast not made payments for tender loaned against thy mark. Such failure resulteth in all items in thy possession being forfeited."

I directed mine attention to Hassid. "How could this come to pass?"

"I tried thine ear but found it deaf. The carpenter sold his tool. When I mentioned thy displeasure with it, he made available the design to entrants hither and yon. Thy rivals have brought goods at much lower prices to market. The masses have not as keen a sense as thee and are willing to take the lesser quality for the reduced cost. Thy competitors have carved significant positions in the marketplace by offering their cheap goods. The incredible savings that were provided made it impossible to compete. I lowered our prices, but earnings soon transformed to losses. I responded by taking on debts that became thine undoing."

"I am in utter disbelief. My thriving operation hath been demolished. How cruelly fortune turns! Please leave me be, I must reflect."

The usurer and his soldiers milled about, collecting mine equipment and records. I left the scene a dejected man. 'Tis better never to obtain prosperity than to do so and have it appropriated.

The next few days were spent fasting and meditating in an attempt at introspection. I would do so seated on the hillsides overlooking the Vale of Oorjit. As the third sun of my fast arose, I witnessed a curious sight. 'Twas Nasir in the valley below, releasing a falcon from the perch of his forearm. I descended the slope to greet him as the gray bird soared in the majestic skies above.

"Thou art a falconer as well, Nasir?"

With his back turned he quipped, "Among other pursuits." The falcon plunged into the valley and replaced itself on his extended arm, shaking its head, stretching its wings and then tucking them. "I have searched for thee, as I have heard talk in the territory that thou hast lost thy livelihood. What I do not comprehend is why this news cometh to me from common folk and not from thee."

"I elected not to burden thee. After three days of meditation, I have determined that I must avoid risk."

"Nonsense. That is the nature of trade, for the tradesman and purchaser alike. As a merchant, thou takest risks in pursuit of profit, whilst thy patron placeth his faith in thee. Thy mark representeth thy warranty, whether written or implied," he admonished. The falcon bristled at Nasir's animated state. Having forgotten that the pet was perched on his limb, he set the bird to the wind once more.

"Life is but a test of perception. She pointeth out thy weaknesses and exploiteth them till thou art either fortified or shattered," Nasir counseled. "Thy failure repeated itself in a number of ways so that thou mightest become aware. First, thine inability to respond in a timely manner birthed thy loss. By adjourning decisions that warranted prompt action, thou allowed a seemingly minor dilemma to augment into calamity.

"Thy lack of innovation caused thee to lapse further," he continued. "Thou hast been warned that initiatives showing promise become hunted. Yet thou had not the vision to perfect the carpenter's apparatus. Hubris impaired thy judgment, making thee imagine time would wait for thee, a common miscalculation.

"Thy third indiscretion was placing responsibility in another who was inexpert," Nasir said. "Once thy workman proved himself unqualified, thou neglected to remove him. In so doing, a critical situation became dire. The cumulative price paid was the weakening of thy mark beyond repair.

"As troubles gain momentum, one must act decisively. Every failure to act may be countered with a decisive action twice its force. Consider a footrace, for instance. Should one find himself trailing behind, one must run doubly fast in order to overtake the lead. This being said, with what actions shalt thou opt to correct these missteps?" he asked in conclusion.

"I have no compass with which to decide a path."

"Humankind will pardon thee if thou mistakest thine actions, but never will it forgive thee if no decision is made on thy part. Thou canst not always react properly in accordance to thy circumstances, for thou art mortal. However, when the situation is fully understood, thy pronouncement should come within a span of seven breaths. Practicing decisive action will develop in thee a more potent, constructive moral fiber, one that will hold a stronger magnetism to those in concordance with thine own. Success is ultimately certain if thou makest enough decisions and enactest them to thine utmost capability. Dost thou deem thy proprietorship one worthy of resurrection?" he questioned.

"I do. No competitor knoweth more of oils than I, nor can any incorporate the wisdom I have accrued. Test my will and I shall show thee my resolve. The trade shall be raised anew, never to succumb from a failure to act decisively again," I proclaimed.

Nasir nodded with approval.

* * *

The Baron and his adherents arrived at the renowned Fane of the Ascetics late in the day. As he cleverly explained the insight his pupils should take from the lecture, they climbed a stairway that had been carved naturally into the face of a cavernous mountain centuries past. Upon entering the academy, they bypassed a long queue of hopeful ascetics that had collected atop the steps tarrying overlong for the opportunity to study in the fane. After several days' wait, the rust-colored iron doors that concealed the coveted teachings swung open. A young group of novices in white robes poured out, carrying wooden buckets of fresh water and steaming brown rice. They hurriedly placed the pails at the top of the stairs and rushed back through the doors, closing them tightly. Many of the prospects raced to the provisions. Some waited their turn, whilst others chose no sustenance at the time. One of the elders came from within the institute to observe the potential candidates. He was dressed in a saffron-colored habit and ornamented with gold bands on each of his muscular arms. The aging master paid particular attention to those who remained calm and denied the offerings. After a few moments of contemplation, he carefully dismissed those who had failed to exhibit strength of will, allowing only two aspirants entrance.

Beyond the iron doors stood a large earthen courtyard. Hefty stone figures of notable founders from generations past were in each corner of the quadrangle. More impressive still were the dozen ascetics in purple garb that encircled Wali, who stood in the center, dressed in a black cowl.

The Baron and his students quietly watched the ascetics engage Wali in a martial exercise. One by one and subsequently in groups, they made attacks upon his person. Wali adroitly unbalanced the first by sweeping his foot. He then used his assailant's forward momentum to toss him to the ground. Without hesitation, a second combatant attacked from behind, locking Wali's neck in the crook of his arm. Wali sensed the danger immediately, grabbed his attacker's arm, leaned forward with straddled legs, and sent his opponent tumbling over him to the packed earth. Yet a third challenger attacked with a punch. In one swift movement, Wali parried the blow, closed the distance between them, then rendered his provoker to the dirt. There he applied a stranglehold, causing the ascetic to urgently tap Wali's shoulder in submission.

"Allowing one's education to lead to sensible action will naturally yield richness, for scholarship without application is imprudent," remarked the Baron whilst Wali continued to spar. After adjusting his garments, the Baron questioned thus, "Before I part to converse with the elders, what have you ascertained this day?"

They contemplated his appeal several moments. "One doth not meet his ruination all at once, but through a series of minor infractions that mount and descend upon him," acknowledged Mbolaji. "Things of import need not become pressing. Problems may be quelled if one acteth decisively. On the contrary, to dawdle bringeth about one's undoing. He who doth not slay this mentality thwarteth himself. Most great events, be they triumphs or disappointments, began as seeds. Kingdoms are fostered over many generations."

After much care, Tunde came forward. "Resolute action, combined with strength of will, creates an irresistible force. With it, one reduceth mountains to rubble. It mattereth not how much confidence one possesseth, nor how many brilliant ideas he deviseth. In the end, the ability to act decisively seteth one apart from mediocrity."

"So long as one is adept, one is capable of acting decisively," Khaleef interjected. "For each failure, a corrective action of twice the magnitude should be prescribed. Moreover, one should seek to resolve problems with a different philosophy than when they were fashioned; one must think on a larger scale to act decisively bolder. To discount this tenet is most unwise."

SHINING

The sun rose as the Baron finished running around the outskirts of the estate, his physical conditioning for the morn. As he wiped his brow of dense sweat with a piece of cambric, he greeted his prentices in the study of the western wing which was shaded from the daystar. The students' attention, however, lay upon the immense ancient language key that spanned the entirety of the longest wall in the chamber. It was papyrus, manipulated by a rope and pulley that circulated from the floor to the ceiling.

"Preceptor, what is this enormous text?" inquired Mbolaji.

"It is the decipherment of tongues from the many lands surrounding us. This is how I am able to effectively communicate with our far-reaching brethren. I make certain to reference it, lest I go misunderstood by those in attendance at Parliament."

Wali directed servants as they offered a selection of fruits and freshly pressed nectars. Tunde politely turned down Wali's offer of sustenance. The others graciously followed.

"'Tis uncouth to refuse the offerings of thine host," said Wali.

"If I have offended mine instructor, please accept my most humble apology," said Tunde. "In the midst of learning, I find it best to deny myself food. When I partake, vital fluids leave my brain to assist in digestion. I merely wish my faculties to be their sharpest."

The Baron warned of the long day ahead and advised that they nourish heartily, even if they found it distracting at first. "Nutriment protecteth you from exhaustion. Proper fare serveth to instill in you that the body must be as finely tuned as the mind. This is a necessary practice to incorporate. Do note, an alteration in one's spoon victuals helpeth not a man who doth not redirect his thoughts." The Baron turned his attention to include the rest of his disciples. "Have ye any questions thus far?"

"Indeed, counselor, we are eager to know how ye once again amassed your considerable fortune. Such stories give mine own dreams promise and strengthen my will," said Mbolaji.

"Very well then," the Baron replied. "Pay close attention; I will assist you in differentiating magnates from tradesmen." The Baron summoned Wali to fetch water basins so they could all wash their faces and hands. Wali then motioned for servants to have these placed before them.

"Gather your scrolls," the Baron declared, "for after I refine myself, we shall journey to the regional forum where court advisors debate current societal issues. One man mighteth hold the power of many when the maxim I shall divulge there is understood."

* * *

Strangely enough, I had lost everything for the second time in life, yet was not crestfallen. I felt not humbled, but challenged by Destiny. These events confirmed that the trials of life are simply a contest to judge one's will.

I sought Nasir, for with his assistance I was assured I could register a prudent strategy.

The fourth sun of my search arose, and I found Nasir fishing for breakfast in the River Taliv. This was an odd sighting; I had searched for him in town to no avail, only to discover him when I least expected.

"Nasir, pray, lend me thine ear. I am without the proper resources to resurrect my trade. Of more pressing concern is the potential inability to compete with an idea that hath progressed beyond mine own mastery."

"How dost thou propose to contend whilst the advantage is firmly in thy rivals' grasp?" Nasir queried as he checked his line.

"I shall convince my men to work twice as hard and long as mine adversaries!"

He chortled at my boastful response and then lunged for his rod as it flew into the river. Watching his pole be carried off downstream, he asked, "And what shall that accomplish but tiresome days and exorbitant costs from extended wages? Dilemmas resolved with four days of physical labor may be remedied in one day of resourceful thinking. Seek not to solve predicaments using toil; hard work alone accomplisheth naught. Prescribed is inventive, concentrated foresight. Query thyself to ease thine efforts in multiplying yield. Didst thou find thy customer appreciating all aspects of thy presentation? Which facet of operations accounted for thy major cost? Which fragrance yielded the most profit?"

I could not answer these questions without consulting my scrolls. Recognizing my vacillation, Nasir continued, "Unwise men focus on all portions of their lives uniformly, when such equilibrium cannot be found. Even amid that which is similar, there is always a dominant component."

A moment of clarity. "Thou art suggesting that I center on the details that dearly affect my success. I should improve the processes that achieve maximum yield. 'Twould also be wise to reduce costs associated with the larger expenses and concert mine efforts toward fragrances that account for the most sales. Further, I must court patrons who purchase the lion's share of merchandise. 'Tis with these means my trade shall once again find its glory."

"And what of the carpenter's tool?" Nasir queried.

"I shall render it of little import. The factor of differentiation shall be the attentiveness that is placed into our handmade goods. The distinction in quality shall be enough to justify the inflated price when public notice hath been heightened."

Finding Nasir left me agog for seedling capital. First I pursued the usurers hither and thither, but they all were aware of my situation and chose only to refuse me. These failed attempts instilled in me the determination to raise funds from a private gold lender.

I relied on the services of Rawan, who was proving to be more of an asset every day. I shared my concerns pertaining to my lack of resources. He then alerted me to a prince named Farad of Solat. He was the most recent member of royalty to place an order for exclusive oils made from a rare orchid hybrid Rawan had created. Farad was known to be a man of discernment and commercial exploits. I agreed that he seemed at the very least a capable referral, so I allowed Rawan to request his attention on my behalf. Upon his return one moon later with the prince's acceptance of mine arrival, I traveled the seventeen-day trek to the peninsula of Solat at the southwesternmost part of the country.

Farad's retinue greeted me at the gates of his manse and escorted me to a bathing pool. Once I was thoroughly cleansed, the prince sent his servant to bring me before him in the drawing room. Potted orchids of all species, some of which were unfamiliar, cleared the black granite path that I followed to a large table with cushions surrounding its feet. Orchids even intertwined the wrought-iron window frames. Upon mine entrance, tropical birds twittered and flapped their wings against the bars of gilded cages placed atop black granite stands.

Prince Farad entered shortly after. He was tall and wiry, with a nose that protruded from his long oval face. He spake with a nasality most people from the peninsula incorporated in their dialect. He affirmed, "If thou art capable of withstanding the Scroll of Indagation I have prepared for thee, I shall agree to negotiate further and potentially finance thine endeavor." The same retinue that greeted me earlier directed a multitude of servants to deliver Farad's volumes of scrolls. They placed them in neat piles to my right and left. With that, the prince exited, followed by his servants. Promptly, the room was secured so that I might begin my review unmolested.

I unrolled the first manuscript and read the opening question. "How many men hast thou queried in search of a partner in trade?"

On a blank scroll, I scribbled mine answer with one of the quills and ink provided me: "In excess of three hundred, to date."

It took six suns to complete his course. Even if I did not win his purse, he had won my deference. The prince posed an endless list of questions, some of which I never would have considered otherwise. In his survey were certain fundamental queries, such as:

357. Characterize thy behavior, attitude, and approach to life. How do they conjoin?
423. What is thy style of leadership?
462. What are the various barriers for new entrants?
514. Is thy product in a new, emerging, mature, or declining stage?
   a. Dost thou know the density of the market?
   b. What is the rate of growth per annum for each product? State thy projections.
589. What achievements hast thou made?
   a. How successful were they, and why?
630. How are thy goods priced, and how do they compare with those of thy competitors?
   a. Who are thy major contenders, and what are their financial strengths?
705. What production changes are intended?
712. Which variables are key in the decision to purchase thy product?
765. Is loyalty exhibited from thy customers?
   a. What factors affect their need for thy product?
   b. What would cause an increase or decrease in need?
794. What is required to persuade patrons of a challenging product to switch to yours?
795. How many alternatives do the patrons have?
801. Identify thy management strengths.
816. What are thy strategic advantages?
837. Detail the direst risks in backing thy venture.

To many of his queries I had no answers at first. To others, my written replies seemed unfavorable. I answered honestly and to the best of mine ability. All that was left to give was my confidence. I trusted that it would be not solely mine answers that interested him, but the nature of my responses.

Prince Farad perused my replies whilst I rested during the seventh sun. 'Twas on the eighth day of my stay that I was brought before him once again in the room of orchids. Seated on cushions, we faced each other across the large, circular agate table. Farad debated, "Doth not the rejection of so many men only prove the notion that thine endeavor seemeth implausible?"

"I am not the reason such men lack heart. They simply know not of the riches lying in wait. They reject only mine ideas, not wealth. Every man that resisteth mine entreaty bringeth me closer to acceptance. Somewhere there is a man with dreams of achievement the same as mine own. He will be found."

"Yes. But what if thou art not able to find a financial partner? How long would thy search continue?"

"Till there is not a man walking the earth who knoweth not my name. After every man of means hath received and denied me, I shall approach each man again. Those days of rejection may have merely been inauspicious ones. I shall repeat this process until my vision is brought to fruition or my body holdeth no breath."

"Then thou wouldst allow nothing to stop thee," Farad surmised.

"Indeed, my will is already done. I need only realize it."

"I see. Many of thine answers were not ideal, Merchant, but neither were they chimerical. This inquisition was just as much a probe of thy character as of thy business. Investments are not courtships, they are marriages."

"Upon our first meeting, didst ye not pass judgment on my moral fiber?" I asked.

"In prior dealings with those who have come before me, I have learned that to pass judgment prematurely is unwise. Scores of men, upon first glance, appear unable to face mine examination. If he is a man of affluence, his presentation might reveal his attention to detail. To those unacquainted with the study of character, if he is of modest means, his tattered garb might tarnish him. The Scroll of Indagation revealeth a man's true nature, regardless of the garments he weareth."

Farad continued, "The ways of exchange measure men by seven elements: character, vision, competence, will, values, associations, and successes. Unethical men shall not receive gold from me regardless of how they may rank in the other areas. Shortsighted men achieve small victories at best; thus, they should occupy lesser posts. Incompetent men should never be hired. If, in due course, one is found, his overseer's prudence should be called into question as well. Men with weak will are unable to persist through difficult times, whilst a man whose values differ from yours will promote discordant causes.

"If a man possesseth the first five elements, one needeth not be concerned with the last two, they shall find him. They serve to gauge how mature in the ways of trade one is. The more mature, the lower the risk of monetary loss."

Farad sipped some tea before saying, "There are those who stake their fortunes on men with no history of accomplishment. I am not of their ilk. To wager on a new venture carrieth the largest reward, and with it equal peril. I prefer to limit untoward possibilities. My judgment is respected, and any man in whose character I believe may mention my mark to lords and lenders alike.

"Upon review of thine answers, I reckon thou art a man in possession of the first five elements. A young, enterprising man sound of mind and body, with confidence and wisdom, is rarely found. I deem thee to be a worthy associate in which to venture in a business that holdeth mine interest. Under terms that the product line concentrate on scents that have yielded the most success, coupled with the use of the latest tools, I would agree to an equal partnership," Farad finished.

Astonished, I was able to muster, "Thank you, Prince, for this chance to show mine ability. I shall not fail."

"I believe in thee, Merchant."

Farad sent word to three paymasters who, prior to his acquaintance, had denied me capital. I then summoned Rawan and we went to see Hassid's carpenter friend. I was apologetic in mine appeal and was able to commission him to build a new version of his tool. Considering his recent success, I was surprised at how receptive the carpenter was to an individual who had refused him once before; he had been given no reason to be kind to me. He further extended his services by describing the problems many of my competitors had experienced with his initial design. It took us days to study and refine. Upon completion of our apparatus, I possessed a machine superior to those of my competitors. In two moons I was ready to summon my workforce once more.

We focused intensely on aspects of our business that affected our survival the most. The application of the innovative device substantially reduced the cost of operations. This allowed more time to concentrate on items with the highest margins of profit. We centered on capturing market share from competitors who had the most patrons. Jalaal assisted me with special marketing strategies to capture purchasers who would buy the most in one visit. To gain these people as loyal customers by catering to their needs would prove fortuitous. Finally, after much trial and error, my workforce and I were successful in mastering that which previously was our demise.

Within nine seasons mine oil became the most widely acclaimed. Since the improved device operated three times faster than those of my competition, I was able to supply more consumers at a faster rate. Again, I was in demand by nobility and peasantry. Farad prospered handsomely, as did I, more so than before. He would defer to my judgment on most subjects. I proposed to call on my competitors in an effort to purchase their marks. It would allow them to exit the trade with some coin in their purses rather than none.

On the agreed-upon date, I received them in Solat. I entered the meeting dressed in nothing less than the finest robes fashion allotted, and was bedecked in jewels of the highest caliber. 'Twas apparent from my dress that I had been gifted with prosperity. Seated around the black agate table in the room of orchids, the other proprietors, who had fallen on hard times as I carved into their customer bases, were begrudging as they set eyes upon mine attire. When the negotiations ended, I had successfully bargained for the ownership of every one of my competitors' operations. After paying them fairly, I stood as the sole marketer of my chosen goods.

Nasir surprised me with a visit to mine operation in Solat the following sun.

"The masses celebrate thy service. Thou hast successfully created a need in the public. Thy mark is firm in legend," Nasir stated.

"I have been provided with good fortune once again."

"Why dost thou think this is so?"

"It is due to the understanding of what holdeth importance for mine advancement," I answered. "By focusing on the consequential, critical tasks have proven little challenge. I am able to accomplish far more. Time spent on menial errands hath been reduced fivefold. It amazeth me how quickly I have been able to multiply all things I value."

"Hast thou found any other uses for such a power?"

"With most things, especially in my relationships."

"Please explain," Nasir requested.

"I objectively viewed mine interactions with those around me, be they friends or business partners. I pushed myself to find value in each relationship. Some provided a listening ear, others, new information. Several fostered alliances with men of significance. Upon identifying the true value in a certain affiliation, I chose to do everything possible to add to that particular aspect," I replied.

"Might I ask, what didst thou find?"

"Mine observations were twofold. Whilst concentrating on adding value to various relationships, I noticed an imbalance. Despite having several associations, 'twas a small percentage that actually added value to mine existence. Many robbed me of my life force and financial strength. I became aware of men who cost silver every time I looked upon their faces. Their swift and changeable manners were that of serpents, yet I remained unmoved. I eased out of contacts that drained me, and alerted myself to relationships that emboldened my person."

"Dost thou mean to say thou wouldst terminate a bond that brought favor to another rather than thyself?"

"Indeed not. I asked myself whether the effort I place into a certain person is appreciating and thereby worth the energy I am exerting. Will this seed I am planting have a more fruitful yield for either my counterpart or myself? If the answer was favorable, I continued to focus on the relationship. Many were inapt for prenticeship, though their objectives were honest. If a man was not prepared, I lessened my time spent in his presence until life gave him more perspective to fully appreciate our exchange."

"What result hath this yielded?" he asked.

"Quite a profitable one. A few men's productivity out-shineth all others. They understand the need to accomplish the work of multiple men in less time. Their effectiveness is without equal and, when combined with mine, becometh an unconquerable force. By incessantly concentrating on our strengths, we became more efficient."

"Thou must be pleased with these new insights."

"Nay," I replied, "they have further incited the fire burning within. I found that the size of an operation mattered not. By observing the outcomes of small shops, results could be prefigured for larger operations as well. Minding this principle gave life a certain foretelling quality."

"And what are the implications of such a revelation?" Nasir provoked.

"If one could successfully identify the methods most important to any given trade, isolate them for creative analysis, then share the results with other proprietors, one could receive a portion of that merchantry for leading such vendors to higher profits," I affirmed.

Nasir clapped his hands in a congratulatory gesture of approval.

"I loathe curtailing our exchange, Nasir, yet I wish to share these insights with Farad." We spake our parting words then I rushed to find the prince.

Once I met with Farad, I suggested that we try to reproduce our success in other areas of commerce. He entertained the idea momentarily but, being a conservative man, recommended we continue with what had made us so successful. He felt that an expansion into other businesses carried an undue risk. Reluctantly, I acquiesced.

I continued to operate successfully with profits showing persistent growth over the seasons. There were more than one thousand men in various regions representing me. With the exception of those serving kings, no other person employed more. This increased mine influence in the territories. Farad's involvement caused royal families to charge him with trying to usurp the resources of their kingdoms by means of trade. This became a very thorny situation to discern and required skilled negotiation to maintain pleasant relations.

The brewing political issues proved no contest with the violent forces of nature. Our region faced unusually severe droughts for several moons. Water was scarce and thus brought hardship on the people, eventually forcing shops to close. The once fruitful province became a wasteland, and Patlaan savages from the north periodically made attacks on townspersons in search of provisions. The cost of everyday necessities soared drastically due to the struggles in the region. Our strategies kept us afloat for a while, until the floodwaters finally came. The heavens had greedily reserved the source of life for moons at a time, then suddenly let it loose in torrents. The deluge wiped out every business, leaving nothing above water. Each plant fortunate enough to survive the drought under the protective watch of our employees had since been waterlogged, and no longer emitted its characteristic potency.

The townspeople had lost much and were in no position to purchase anything. We began sustaining losses, and eventually Farad beseeched me to buy his position in the operation. He wanted to move on, but I was not quite ready to give up. I offered the prince a sizable portion of gold for his interest in the mark. He accepted a significantly discounted sum for exiting during such tumultuous conditions. Farad viewed his position as he did any other loss he incurred over the years: as one to be managed. To me it defined my being. For days it rained, forcing those who could to seek high ground. Albeit I was able to remain open during a terrible drought followed by a flood, it became apparent that mine efforts were in vain. I had not sold a vial of fragrance in almost four moons and could not recoup the monies paid to the prince. My business was no more and I had once again contributed to its demise.

My circumstances prompted me to seek Nasir's counsel. He had never proved a simple man to locate when I wanted an audience of him. I was certain he was no longer in Solat as I had not seen him recently. I made the seventeen-day journey back to Daibae. I was without anyone and anything, as even my brethren had lost all faith in my capabilities as a leader. I went to the Vale of Oorjit in case Nasir might be there, letting his bird stretch its wings. As the sun awakened a new day, I was able to locate Nasir, perched high in the branches of a eucica tree. It was dense with green almond-shaped leaves that shone silver when breezes cooled them. Eucica fruit was said to increase the duration of life and improve mental faculties. 'Twas only fitting to find him partaking of its sweet, yellow, fleshy meat.

"Thy person seemeth troubled. What aileth thee?" asked Nasir, untangling from his perch to level himself with me.

"My resolve hath been tested once again. Thrice mine attempts have been berated, and I have been stripped of my whole lot," I said bitterly.

"I see. Hold not to disappointment, for the wise know that as in games of chance, neither good fortune nor hardships endure without end. True warriors celebrate peace yet thrive in battle. 'Tis the same for masters of trade who rejoice in abundance, yet prove their resolve in times of adversity and monetary struggle."

"Whilst drought and flood battered the southwestern regions, many tradesmen were robbed of their spirit, not to mention their wealth. As for me, I could not help but be amazed at the speed with which Fortune turned against me. She hath thrown numerous challenges my way to strengthen my will. Her lessons have been cruel yet effective from lifetimes of dealing with men in pursuit of power. The lesson taught me at this turn was shining: to focus on what is most important in every instance. This will help me predict the outcomes of the circumstances into which I am thrust, making my success a certainty."

"If triumph be thy true desire, establish what thoughts served thee well or led thee astray," Nasir advised.

"Clearly, shining hath increased mine effectiveness and shown considerable yield. By exercising focus I rebuilt my trade with a fraction of the effort in notably less time. To resurrect another should take little exertion. At present, this insight is my most valuable guide. I have failed only in protecting myself from catastrophe."

* * *

The gathering was held on the mall near Lake Inor. The Baron and his scholars positioned themselves within earshot of the crowd. There were four and twenty delegates in all, one pair representing each territory in the civilized world. The different tongues spoken blended to create an incoherent drone and were heard behind the Baron's distinctive voice.

"Observe the dynamics of this collective. Ye will find men of various expertise, but within this group some will dominate the exchange of views, depending upon the subject matter being appraised. Pay close attention, for more will be withheld than is revealed."

"Whatever dost ye mean?" Khaleef asked.

"In matters of governance, men will suppress their true

motives. 'Tis imperative that one differentiate between one who is silent due to lack of knowledge and one who remaineth hushed because he secretly plotteth. The difference may be quickly ascertained by well-placed questions. If answers from the former seem blasphemous, he is genuinely ignorant. If the latter equivocateth in his response, 'tis he who conspireth for his own betterment."

Tunde made an interesting pronouncement. "The depth of your understanding of the outlying regions alloweth you to see more clearly what these advisors neglect with the narrow concerns of their provinces. By perceiving their shortcomings, ye art able to profit from their oversights."

The Baron smiled at how well the students were taking to his lessons.

Tunde continued, "I can see a predictive quality in examining the influential voice behind the policy of a king. To position yourself where ye knowest there is soon to be opportunity must yield profit."

"What other comments have ye of import from all ye have seen and heard mentioned?" the Baron tested.

"That there is a distinct relationship between the contributions of people, places, and circumstances. A few contributors, more often than not, have a disproportionate effect on the amount produced," Tunde said.

"Effectiveness may be multiplied if one concentrateth on the vital components of a situation that have bearing on one's desired result. Any seed I wish to see burgeon can become so with focus," said Mbolaji.

"Shining enhanceth every interaction. The exchanges that increase the strength of a bond will flourish as a result of one's influence," Khaleef affirmed. "'Tis far wiser to improve these relationships than spend time on lesser interactions that squander one's days."

"I cannot find flaw with any of these," the Baron approved. He ordered Wali to bring the horses.

The pupils continued their discussion well into the night. After each was certain he would not forget this lesson, the students decided it best to make ready for the following day.

SUPREME PRINCIPLE SIXTH

AGGRANDIZE OR RUINATE

"trust ye are well rested, scholars, for we have an all-inclusive day ahead of us," the Baron declared.

The pupils followed their enlightener through the long halls of the residence and down a flight of stairs that led to the cookroom. The wall nearest the entrance was lined with copper pots and ladles of all sizes. The scullery was home to an immense brick oven filled with flat dough starting to rise. The smells that emanated from that afternoon's batch were enough to excite any palate. Two cooks stood over a steaming kettle; one stirred its contents whilst the other poured chopped vegetables from a bowl into the cauldron. In the farthest corner of the room, the learners set their eyes upon an extraordinary contraption meant to keep perishables chilled until they were ready for consumption. As the students pulled the latch of the box, they found fresh fish caught earlier that morn and still smelling of the ocean, covered in ice shipped from the north. They marveled awhile at the unusual device until they heard a loud thud in yet another corner.

Two cooking assistants were engaged in a game of knife throwing. They targeted a small circular wooden board hanging some five and ten hands from the ground on the wall facing the students. With a smirk, the Baron unsheathed a paring knife from a wooden holder on a side table. He quickly took aim and hurled the blade through the space between the players' heads, completely to their astonishment. The Baron had outscored them both, and from a farther distance, proving himself no stranger to this diversion. His skill was met with applause. The Baron then excused his servants and made ready to prepare a special meal.

When his cooks parted, the Baron instructed the students to pick vegetables from the pantry and dice them. Khaleef laughed when Mbolaji fumbled in his attempt to chop a head of red cabbage.

The Baron directed his attention to his troubled prentice. "Be cautioned against a lack of focus in unfamiliar situations. However, fret not. Precision is learned and shall come with diligence.

"Blind consumption of victuals is injurious to the human form. One must be intimate with one's diet in order to regulate its effect on one's health. As I recount to you today's lesson, ye shall prepare your first meal so ye might learn of the foods ye intake."

"Our minds have been ever active since our first night here. We are alert and prepared for your tutelage," said Mbolaji.

"Excellent. Let us begin then." The Baron seated himself in front of the students. In turn they took to their stools around the butcher block and made ready to absorb his precepts. "Personal insight can be disrupted by outside forces, yet its true power is broken solely by oneself. Within is the potential to become one's own minder or nemesis.

"'Tis the repetition of specific measures that alloweth one to unconsciously duplicate successes or failures. Notice how a man's schedule reflecteth his thoughts. Just as one's body hath matters of course, so shall one's mind. Take care, however, for a duality lieth therein. With this concept, a man's actions serve either as the marble to erect his empire or iron bars to fit his prison.

"Heed, for misapplication of this axiom is not easily reversed. Yet the magnitude of its effects can only be observed with Time's passage, for 'tis she who giveth routine its sway or maketh the tethers that bind one. If misused, one will not notice her bondage until the consequences become burdensome."

* * *

"Industrious one, thou hast already modified thy behavior," said Nasir. "Still, 'tis necessary that thou make more apparent the variances to improve thy trade. I shall open thine eyes to the contrariety between individuals that shall most impact thy livelihood. Thou mightest observe that the major differences are created through their mores," Nasir elucidated as I shadowed his movements through the marketplace, a bustling arena of commercial dealings. "I shall reveal to thee the differences between those who are affluent and those who are destitute, those whose lives reflect peace and those who live in constant turmoil. Among them thou wilt also find men of sound mind and body versus those who are plagued with continuous sickness."

"Do a man's practices carry such weight in all aspects of his existence?" I inquired.

"Certainly. Monitor the total condition of a man's life. Thou shalt notice that the preponderance of his accomplishments as well as his afflictions stem from recurring mental processes."

We discreetly observed many different types of people throughout the region. We encountered two couples; the women from each pair were with child.

"Examine the interactions between both pairs and tell me thy prediction for the life of each unborn child."

As Nasir instructed, I took notice from afar of the two couples' interactions for several days. The first couple often argued when facing unforeseen crises. With each difficult situation came an apparent further loss of spirit. In contrast, the second couple sat peaceably to talk and plan. Every so often they smiled and laughed together. This pair seemed much happier on the whole. Even when confronted with challenging situations they remained unruffled.

I rejoined Nasir after completing my task. "For the first child, I prophesy struggle in all his knotty dealings, whilst the second shall bear a much easier load."

"How didst thou come to such a conclusion?"

"'Tis apparent the first couple viewed circumstance with trepidation," I responded. "The probability of their child adopting a similar tendency is high, in mine humble opinion. He would likely become averse to risk for fear of loss and shun prospects of opportunity. He might also develop an accursed low image of self."

"And of the second?"

"The second couple regarded situations from a positive vantage point, having optimistic expectations. They prepared for hardship and complained not, nor did they allow dire incidents to consume them. Their offspring would more likely embrace calculated risk and, in doing so, be more apt to find success."

"I hope thou understandest this principle fully after effecting this assignment," Nasir began. "A man's habits begin not with him, but with his father. For whatever rituals paternal figures might carry out, be they good or bad, they must be reviewed shrewdly, so as to keep from passing negativity on to their progeny."

"Art thou saying one cannot alter the conditions of his life that were projected upon him by his environment?" I inquired.

"Quite the contrary. Whilst 'tis true that parents must be mindful during a child's formative years, 'tis only with a developed conscience that one is able to filter out negative influence. Only when a child matureth into adulthood will he be equipped to combat the influences of his past. Remember that this capability is formed not in the passing of one day, but of many. 'Tis the father's debt the scion is forced to repay. Therefore, the bonds from years of negative influence take time to break. Allow this example to remind thee that one must be heedful of the environment he createth, for it affecteth not only him, but other generations to come."

"I know and understand."

"Good. Now come with me and I will show thee two other people. Again, I assign thee to study their actions."

He took me to a riparian shantytown where I was to observe two indigent men. I carefully surveyed their actions and listened to their exchanges from an appropriate distance. I remained there from midday to moonrise. Once the orb of night passed over mine observation point, I sought Nasir farther down the river's edge, to report my findings.

"The first man's words carried tones of hopelessness and antipathy. He spake of all objectives as being impossible to reach. He showed resentment for men of privileged circumstances, yet seemingly hath made no attempts to change his condition thus far. If he maintaineth such practices, fortune shall forever evade him." I sat beside Nasir and watched him skip stones across the shallow, pristine water. The methodical rhythm of the stones breaking the surface had a soothing effect, which further helped to clear mine head.

"'Tis widely accepted that a man who striveth not to improve himself shall have everything he holdeth dear taken away. Growth and advancement go rewarded, whilst listlessness and decline are severely punished. If a man stagnateth whilst his brother matureth, the world will celebrate the latter's mark in victory and shun the former's indolence. If one's being were to languish, he would surely die. So too, shall a man perish from society if he doth not strive to improve his station. Men seek not the association of the indigent and destitute, except in acts of charity. Even then, the barren shall be cast away if they desire not to progress." Nasir stopped to chew on a blade of tall grass. He then picked up another rock. "What of the second man?"

"Though he filled a lowly post, this man entertained thoughts of majesty. He carried a lofty air about him whilst reading scrolls from wise men past. The pauper ruminated over the missives, scribbling notes on tattered scraps of papyrus. He planned his actions with precision, working diligently in preparation to realize his potential. If he keepeth such practices, Fortune will surely find him."

"There are those who infinitely quote the doctrines of sages, yet they starve, having acted not to benefit from such knowledge and wisdom. The consistent reading of scrolls is seldom enough to attain triumph; one must repeatedly take action toward that aim," admonished my tutor.

"The first man succumbed to predilections that weakened his mind, thus robbing his body. His obese frame evidenced his propensity to consume low-quality foodstuffs in excess. As a result, he suffered ailments that affected his ability to enact ambitions. The man would attempt to escape his problems, seeking refuge in gluttony. These vices were no more solutions than a mirage in the desert is water. They further diminished his power to master self. Valuable energy needed to implement constructive action was squandered combating the effects of these unfortunate afflictions.

"The second man strengthened mind and body. He indulged only in fare that properly nurtured his being. He rested adequately, allowing his intuition the time to map answers to his ideas. He exercised to strengthen his body and discipline his mind. Through meditation, he found peace in introspection. These activities provided energy, forging his armor." I picked up a stone and skipped it across the water, mimicking Nasir's movements. 'Twas quite a relaxing activity, I realized.

"Thou art performing well, friend. We shall continue with our next specimens. This go round, I shall present thee with three friends. From modest backgrounds, they have limited formal education, yet Providence hath treated them differently. One is quite distressed, another moderately wealthy, and the last affordeth the lifestyle of a prince. Acquaint thyself with their behaviors and tell me the distinctions in their handling of gold."

The three were easy to locate, as they all happened to be neighbors. I studied their ways for three suns, then brought my report before Nasir. We met in the melon grove near mine habitation.

"The indigent man laboreth for a wage with the butcher and is heavily indebted to paymasters," I said. "The silver coins allotted him were typically used to satisfy debts or purchase goods he could not afford. He made a practice of spending beyond that which he earned, and attempted to remedy his condition with invocation or by engaging in games of chance with hopes of favor. He did not read scrolls or consult knowledgeable men; as a result his state worsened. Destiny had a firm grasp on this man; he should find only liability and misery.

"The man of moderate means, too, laboreth for a small wage, but secureth rents from riparian land he purchased on the Taliv," I continued. "Before paying another for any good or service, he reserveth one-tenth of his earnings for himself. This man avoided speculation and debt; hence, his coffers have been rewarded. Having modest goals hath reaped him a modest profit. This man's behavior should lead him toward comfort and help him survive hard times, yet he is remiss of creativity and taketh not calculated risks. Therefore, he shall never experience copious wealth.

"The prosperous neighbor demonstrated why a small number of men control the magnitude of assets. He plodded not; both men and gold labored in his stead. Seeking the advice of the learned eased his efforts and multiplied his funds. Although he too, carried large sums unpaid for moons on end, he only borrowed when the yield on his investment far outweighed the rate charged by the usurer.

"His security and comfort were firmly established by rents from his land, partnerships, and the successful manipulation of paymasters. But his practice of lateral thinking birthed the majority of his prosperity. This land merchant encountered no problem that could not be solved by his own hand."

Nasir replied, "Men may find modest wealth by utilizing the systems others have founded, yet only through creative endeavors of their own will the scrolls reward them with distinction."

"I understand now. One must create an article or service to be sold in volume to the masses in order to grow in stature. 'Tis this practice that separated the land merchant from the rest. He learned to broaden his points of view and thereby generated proportionate successes. His focus became expediting the recovery of his initial investment in small but steady increments. Soon he produced gold that outweighed his expenditures. With his vast wealth, he now giveth a percentage of his gold and time to aid others in improving their conditions. If this man continueth such discipline, further success will draw closer," I surmised.

"What hast thou noticed to be the common traits among successful men?"

"Each man expelleth negative thinking from his daily life and influenceth his subconscious thoughts through positive reinforcement," I responded. "They believe that laudable success is their destiny from the start, and take proper steps toward achieving it. They align themselves with men who upgrade their circumstances, productive men who influence them to become industrious in turn. They work conscientiously and most important, are resourceful. They seek to employ their earnings rather than squander them. These men are humble in their deeds and fall not victim to the arrogance that causeth others to fail. They are aware that patterns of sensible reasoning will ensure their fates.

"Nasir," I implored, "thou hast shown me how men are differentiated by habitual practice, but how doth one devise a plan to benefit from it?"

"Thou still requirest some instruction?"

I blanched at this remark. Nasir softened upon regarding my deflated expression. "I will not hold thine hand the whole way, young man. However, I will assist thee with this plan, for I admit, 'tis a trying one."

He sat me down under the shade of a fig tree. He patted me on the back with reassurance and handed me some fruit. I tossed it aside in rebellion. He looked at me in scorn and I immediately regretted my display of frustration. Nasir handed me another fig and I took it gratefully. I felt ashamed at showing him such a lack of appreciation. He took a seat beside me and gave an outline that would serve as my plan.

"Thou must understand that consistently positive thoughts and deeds lay one's foundation for success. Study closely what thou hast grown accustomed to in daily life. Identify the destructive practices that bar thee from thy goal. Next, decide which constructive habits counter them in order to direct thine efforts toward a new path. This will equip thee to excavate thine old trail of negativity, whilst positive forethought will pave the way to abundance. Frequently travel this new road so that constructive habit might take hold, and the weeds of thy ruinous ideas cease to grow. This new road's formation proveth most difficult during its infancy. However, realize it taketh the passing of approximately one and twenty suns for new habit-forming practices to inculcate themselves to memory. Once fixed in the mind, they shall compel thee to act prudently and will yield astounding triumphs when brought to fruition. 'Tis of great import to seek methods that ingrain these tendencies. Wait not for the opportunity to present itself, rather set plans that ensure that such occasions will arise.

"Also, remember that although thine old ways might seem easier, they only create hardship. If thou bendest in weakness, thine opposing forces will strengthen. Each time thou rejectest these negative forces, thou wilt bolster thy commitment. Thy resolve shall be enriched until it cannot be moved. All situations men are confronted with stem from their own habits. These practices are a reflection of their thoughts. Men are incapable of concealing their thinking from others; they will always be revealed through action.

"By attentively studying thy behavior, ask, 'Would a prudent individual act thus?' Then thou shalt notice the distinct patterns that lead to success, and others that lead to failure. There are certain behaviors that shall place thee among exemplary leaders, whilst others merely prompt despair. Always be conscious of manipulating the environment in which thou livest. Discern thy patterns and those of successful men in order to reproduce former victories. Realize the importance of reading scrolls that expound on subjects directly related to thine aim.

"Be it further understood that destructive emotional states can be avoided by understanding the events that spawn them. There are men who speak of being in conditions where, for a time, they feel invincible, their movements without error. By comprehending that one may duplicate the circumstances that led to this condition, one can prevent negative emotional states from occurring."

* * *

"Examine the net result of your actions to determine what must change," the Baron stated. He took a sip of nectar from his golden chalice. "And so, faithful prentices, let me see what ye have deciphered from this episode. Khaleef, speak first."

Khaleef set down his piece of bread and cleared his throat of the meal he had carefully prepared for himself. "A man's thoughts are the foundation of his lifestyle. If he should adopt negative thinking, he shall be thwarted at every turn. If he rein-forceth positive thoughts often, he shall reap benefits aplenty."

"Tunde?" the Baron beckoned.

"Pure thoughts produce like behavior. Habits affect one's life in all aspects. Of particular importance are those that in-volve relationships with others. Their tendencies are contag-ious, ergo 'tis important that one carefully choose his asso-ciates. One must therefore use this tenet to reinforce one's definite purpose, and rebuketh all that lies in disaccord with it."

"Excellent. And Mbolaji, what dost thou think?"

"That 'tis better to prepare in one's youth before the per-manence of one's routines have taken hold. For the man who endureth not discipline shall surely regreteth the pain of its disregard. I shall not be ignorant like the man who is reluctant to alter his behavior, yet expecteth the future to reflect his goal. If one electeth to rehearse proactive behavior from an early age, he shall surely rejoice in the years to follow."

"'Tis evident ye possess a firm grasp on the day's session. Continue to master its truth with the rest," the Baron said. "Repeat your definite purpose as ye have done each morn, forming this practice into a habit that shall be ingrained in your memory. Envision your future as vividly as I stand be-fore you. Hold no emotion that might weaken your disposi-tion. Awake every morning and reinforce that which shall hold your definite purpose close. Rest now, and we shall re-convene upon the morrow."

Upon his closing statement, the Baron rose and left the scholars to clean their workplaces whilst ruminating over the day's topic. Tunde was so moved by the Baron's drive that he was compelled to make one last declaration.

"Those who are patient in trivial things and possess total control of self will one day have the same mastery in accom-plishing complicated feats."

THE INSIGHT THAT DECIMATION BRINGETH

t sunrise, Tunde, Mbolaji, and Khaleef hastened to the Baron's study, which had become the room they favored most in his large manse. It truly was a place conducive to learning the keys to successful living. Fascinated by all they had received, the three men rushed up the massive winding staircase from their resting quarters. Where once before it seemed impossible to find unaided, they could now navigate the path to what they termed the "Knowledge Chamber."

Wali greeted them and offered fresh, crisp sheets of papyrus and a new supply of quills. He then invited them to consume some traditional regional fare. As they indulged in stewed fish and quail eggs in coconut milk, yam flour pancakes, and boiled greens of turnips, the Baron entered. He was pleased to see his learners partaking of a meal.

"Good day."

"Excellent, Your Grace," Mbolaji declared.

The Baron waved off Wali's assistance and grabbed a bowl and ladle to draw a portion for himself. He was careful not to spill the steaming liquid and took his place among them.

"After we conclude our nourishment, ye shall learn how one demonstrateth the true nature of one's will. Today I am taking you to a place that holdeth great significance in my life. None of what ye have understood thus far shall matter if ye cannot endure in the face of adversity. Persistence alone is not enough; 'twill only lift you from the sands to challenge again. It will not give you the vantage necessary to persevere. Total command of self is prescribed. To become a luminary, ye must possess a degree of knowledge and understanding sufficient to guide a person or to direct circumstance according to your will. Alert yourselves to subtleties that differentiate success from failure. Even as instructors, ye shall forever remain students, for no situation is exactly the same."

"Then is it persistence combined with discerning experimentation that leads to mastery?" Khaleef interjected.

"Indeed, one must try an infinite number of times to surmount one's circumstance. One cannot acquiesce in the darkest hour when all seems forsaken. In that moment one is as close as one will ever come to changing the plan Fortune hath devised. The more insightful the method employed, the shorter the trail necessary to find achievement. Within every rebuff lieth the opportunity to transcend to a higher level of success if one astutely observeth what the world desireth to teach him," the Baron explained.

"We have observed that with each impediment ye hast faced, ye found more productive ways to better the standard of living for the people," said Tunde. "With this accomplishment came the ability to be of even higher service to others; 'tis a sequence. May we assume that with your latest hindrance, ye also found the opportunity to create value and in turn, more significant rewards?"

* * *

I was diligent in mine attempts to internalize the Laws of Gold; it was the only way I could help anyone again, let alone myself. During these times more than ever, I found it important to consult Nasir.

"Thou art only defeated when thou abandonest thine ambitions," Nasir said as we sat in the shade of the eucica tree. No matter how many times thine advances are thwarted, thou shalt never record a loss if thou refusest to surrender. Even the speculator who wagereth long enough shall receive his due.

"Determination armeth one with the ability to survive any obstacle," Nasir continued. "Thou hast suffered heftier losses than was necessary due to knowing not when to withdraw. If one is careless in his advances, he might not return with the proper resources to mount another assault. Let not emotion cloud thy judgment when curtailing risk. View retreat not as weakness, but as a most intelligent stratagem. Be mindful of the future and all its potential outcomes. Such consideration shall make thee respectful of thy resources and careful of squandering them with ill-laid plans.

"I wish thee to ponder the methods of managing risk. Hazards must be viewed bearing certain considerations in mind. If one's potential losses be sizable, the situation must be mentally pared down in order to manage it more skillfully. No matter how substantial or diminutive one's risks might seem, one should recognize that the peril of loss hath the ability to exacerbate. If thou canst unwind this mystery involving the management of risk, thou shalt be rewarded with a purse that outweigheth all the gold thou hast lost by far. To understand this conundrum to its core shall be the most formidable task thou wilt perform."

I took several days to ponder ideas. So many events had occurred unnecessarily that I was left dumbfounded by my poor decisions. Many of the circumstances thrown upon me could have turned out so differently had I learned from my mistakes. I went to the public bath one day after my daily exercise, sure that I would find my teacher.

"Nasir, I have considered thy proposal and have uncovered many flaws in my venturesome methods. 'Twould be absurd of me to assume total perfection of self. Therefore, I chose several weaknesses that needed the most mending, ones that would also have the most dominant impact upon others.

"As thou hast taught me on myriad occasions in our discussions, if I solve the problems of my brethren, I shall benefit in direct proportion to the value I deliver unto them. Thou hast taught me well that it is not risk that hinders action, but rather fear of its potential detriment. 'Tis human nature to fear loss regardless of possible reward. Mine inability to manage risk poseth a monumental challenge. Hence, its solution should offer a similar recompense."

Nasir asked, "In thine eyes, what do thy brethren fear?"

"They fear death, ill health, and the loss of material possessions. Whilst it may seem that the winds of Fortune determine whether a man shall suffer, 'tis possible to compensate him, to some degree, in gold."

"If, as thou sayest, such apprehension is man's most burdensome obstacle in reaching success, what is the reward for one who easeth another's worriments?"

"His reward shall be as weighty as the gift given," I said.

"What methods hast thou devised to offer such assurances?"

"With time I shall create a system to solve this matter. From reading various scrolls and understanding that all decisions in life mutually affect one another, I have detected certain patterns that replicate themselves throughout nature. With this perception, I can reasonably foresee the percentage of men or businesses that shall be affected by volatility. Because many suffer from similar woes, I shall create a guaranty trade in which men can mitigate risk by paying me a premium to guard against it. By having them contribute small amounts of silver each season, a much larger sum of gold is created in order to compensate a man should he suffer a loss if covered under the terms of our agreement."

"What becometh of the gold?" he asked.

"'Twill remain housed in the trade's coffers. I shall employ it in business transactions and gold lending in order to increase the amount. I will compound the gold in order to multiply earnings, so that it will be sufficient to pay any claim."

"And how mightest thou guard against thine own loss?"

"By appealing to kings and princes of neighboring territories. I shall offer them gold every moon for them to serve as mine assurance. They should agree to receive such an offer since their obligation would be minor, due to it being spread across many kingdoms," I put forward.

"If thine instincts on the demand for such a trade are correct, thou shalt be in possession of a coffer unmatched even to the king's gold lender!" Nasir was truly excited at the prospect that I might accrue such wealth, albeit I had none to speak of at the moment.

His enthusiasm was contagious. I was happy I had finally found what seemed to be an infallible method by which I could help others and myself to the fullest of my capabilities. "With such leverage, there shall be no limitation on trade in the region."

"Thine idea showeth promise, but are there any means by which thou mightest create more value still?" Nasir asked.

"I have considered founding an exchange where merchants and purchasers alike may guard against price fluctuations caused by instability in the supply and demand of commodities. Each person would be able to barter the right to buy or sell those commodities at certain prices on or before a certain day. In turn, for providing this right, the exchange would be compensated with a small sum for each transaction. In time it will be made available on all goods deemed appropriate for such activities."

"Hmm. So people can profit by selling their commodity contract outright or by exercising their respective right to buy or sell on or before the day the contract has expired," he figured.

"Precisely."

After we finished bathing and parted ways, I made plans to meet with Prince Farad. He welcomed me with open arms and held a small celebration in honor of my visit. It had been so long since we last engaged. We briefly recounted our personal ventures in commerce as we strolled his magnificent grounds. We touched on the subject of our partnership from so long ago.

"In retrospect, good Prince, what are your thoughts of our past enterprise?"

"Thou art an honorable man with many talents. Thou hast brought prosperity to my kingdom, not only in gold, but also in positive mental attitude and willingness to share one's blessings. I have learned much through our dealings," he affirmed with a grin.

"I have learned much from you as well. Chiefly my lesson was in the administration of risk. I heeded not your wisdom in abandoning the business when its foundation was unstable."

We reminisced over our experiences and laughed at our follies. After we caught up on the events in Solat, we retired to the drawing room.

"So why hast thou traveled the burning sands to visit with me? If my judgment of thee is correct, thou hast come with a proposal."

I had to chuckle at his perceptiveness. "I have botched all my ventures, yet with each failure came a thorough understanding of commerce and patronage. If in my strides I stumble, I know my destiny requireth that I overcome each challenge. My most recent defeat hath presented me with recognition of how to trounce fear and risk. I have devised several methods by which men may silence fear by hedging their personal and business risks. Be forewarned, my systems will require much of your gold."

Farad patted me on the back encouragingly. "Thou hast mine ear. Please continue. However, understand that our friendship shall have no bearing on the evaluation of thine idea. Thou shalt be subjected to the questions contained within the Scroll of Indagation once more."

"I expect nothing less. Your questions only serve to refine mine own understanding of the idea I present to you. I look at it not as a test, but a process.

"A major factor in hedging risk is to separate emotion from the evaluation of ideas. Prejudice or past relations must not serve to sway a person, or else one shall sacrifice one's gold and commit a disservice to both partners."

I stayed with Farad nearly a fortnight, reviewing the inquiries contained in his scroll. Many of mine oversights came to the fore, uncovered by the interrogation. Prince Farad, after scrutinizing my responses and mulling over the details of the venture, saw the merits of my plan and made the monetary arrangements to implement the idea. We celebrated our new partnership with merriment that very eve. On the last day of my visit, we prepared the necessary measures for distant travel.

We journeyed to various kingdoms and were able to convince much of the aristocracy to function as our assurance. Many were delighted to accept gold every moon against the possibility that a disaster might render their local businesses unable to satisfy their obligations. The droughts and floods of seasons past had taught their lessons well, making for swift negotiations. We then were able to offer the same security to proprietors in nearby regions. Some were skeptical at first. Then over time, several costly incidents occurred that quickly changed their opinions. Tradesmen began to realize that the premium charged was worth the peace of mind they would receive in return.

When our assurance trade established itself as a necessity for businesses and landowners alike, we began to introduce the methods by which merchants could hedge against the movement in prices. What we received in gold from assurances, we earned tenfold through this offering.

We acquired businesses that met the requirements of the Scroll of Indagation with the vast amounts of gold we accumulated. Due to our large reserves, we were able to match the rates offered by the king's gold lenders, allowing us to serve the kingdom's notable patrons. This was a feat no merchant banker had ever achieved. We eventually became so powerful that even kings' usurers partnered with us on developing projects within their territories.

There were merchants who sought to compete with us. The necessary gold required to start a similar business was a large barrier to entry for most. The advantage gained from pioneering an industry was so overbearing, it required a competitor to ally himself with several kings in order to offer prices as low as ours. Smaller, underfunded merchants who unwisely tried to compete with us often saw their coffers run bare in the process.

As word of our enterprise spread, men realized the breadth of services we offered. They took advantage of the convenience of transacting business at one source. We aided them immensely by easing apprehensions and freeing up their reserves. By controlling mountainous sums of gold in every region we occupied, lending rates were forced down, easing the burden of debt on the townspeople. This way, many trades could increase profits and create more posts. Merchants were no longer required to maintain large reserves for their own security; by paying us a small amount of gold for the same assurance, they were able to expand their businesses with funds that previously would have been held in reserve.

Few men were without work, as the prosperity of our trade allowed men to appoint workers and pay higher wages. Those with commercial dexterity borrowed gold from us or would have us be their partners. It was a wonderful position for Farad and me because we were exposed to so many prolific ideas. As honorable men, we only encouraged vendors and never infringed upon them. The exposure to inventive minds provided us with insights to how we might enrich our operations.

Our business, which had now become a large power structure, attracted speculators. As merchants used our exchange to circumvent price volatility, speculators used it to attain short-term profits. As opportunists realized their chances were more certain to make or lose fortunes by purchasing rights and obligations, our business's fame quickly surpassed the more trivial games of chance to which they were accustomed. There were even men for whom speculation became their trade. However, as with all forms of wagering, many sought easy gold with inadequate knowledge and experience. These opportunists found their coffers emptied and their debts augmented. Usually, 'twas the richer, thus more powerful entities that found profit by selling obligations rather than purchasing them. Overall, speculators brought a much-needed element to the exchange; they created liquidity.

I had taken residence in Solat to be closer to Farad's domicile, which served as our exchange's center of operations. Since my relocation, I had not seen Nasir. On the chance he might be in Solat as well, I searched for him in the marketplace whilst purchasing nuts and dried figs. He was not in that stall, so I went in search of him at the lake behind the king's palace. It was a tranquil spot, one I was sure he would visit if in this province.

Mine hunch served me correctly. There he was, preparing to launch a rowboat. He spotted me as I came from behind a large rock formation.

"Friend, thou hast become successful at last. I feel refreshed upon seeing thine happiness. It hath been some time since we last conversed. Come join me on mine expedition and tell me of thy triumphs."

"'Twould be a pleasure." I helped him push the boat into the shallow water. We hopped in, and I took both oars from my guide. "I have heeded thy counsel and have profited tremendously. The knowledge and understanding I have gained through defeat have assisted in honing my thoughts."

"Thou now comprehendest the insight that decimation bringeth. 'Tis unfortunate that many take a nearsighted view when evaluating their actions. As thou well understandest from thine own experiences, man's struggle may not accurately be judged over a short span. Such a limited view shall not allow thee the proper perspective for evaluation. Time shall determine if a man profited from the events that have been presented to him."

"Yes. One must view a man's actions over an extended period. Often it will take ages, or a series of failures, before a man's reward or penalty is revealed," I added with my new-found wisdom.

"'Tis only natural for our lives to stray so that one's ability to thrive might be tested. When Fortune becometh a miser, one can determine if the will to regroup and survive is possessed in him. When she looseneth her grip, one observeth if one hath sufficiently grasped the lessons of defeat, so he might not again be thwarted by similar conditions later. But it is up to each man to determine if he shall learn such a lesson."

"Am I to understand that one mightn't accurately be judged in times of well-being?" I asked.

"Time will prove all ideas no matter what season they come. Confuse not thy genius with the sudden prosperity of the region. True brilliance is seen when one is able to produce gold for others during times of hardship. 'Tis seen when one's deeds willfully slacken Fortune's hand, as thou hast done quite masterfully," he informed. "'Tis difficult times that expose genius, not times of comfort when gain cometh easily.

"If thou art able to ease a man's fear, there is no amount of gold he would not surrender to thee. Because of the marked value thou hast offered thy brethren, thou prospered. Thou hast performed a measureless number of noble deeds that served as a considerable advantage for thee. In addition to offering a needed service, thou hast created one that alloweth people to ease their fears and profit. Thou truly hast answered the prayers of many desperate lives."

Nasir watched me struggle with the oars against the breeze, yet provided no help. He continued, "Though 'tis prudent to think in terms of abundance, what pleaseth me more is that thou hast aided men in guarding against trade declines, and even helped them profit. Because of thee, men thoroughly understand the ways of the world, rather than only possessing a roseate view of it. Thou hast provided men with magnificent options they never had. And consistent with thy most recent concepts, thou taught them to profit from their missteps. Thou hast bestowed upon them the opportunity to conquer failure rather than flee from it."

We came ashore to an islet amid the lake. I pulled the boat from the water as Nasir cleared seats for us to rest. I tethered the rowboat to a nearby tree, then joined my friend under the shade of dense foliage.

"Thou hast always said thy main goal was to finish Qahhar's work and teach the Laws of Gold to the masses," Nasir professed. "How mightest thou create further wealth for thy people?"

"Merchants have expressed interest in acquiring more capital for the expansion of their trades, yet can generate no more debt. I would like to create a method by which people could own a piece of the businesses they patronize. Mine would serve as the vehicle through which men's earnings may be pooled to invest."

"How wouldst thou implement such an idea?"

"I would offer credentials imprinted with our exchange seal. These documents would represent one's ownership in a particular business. That establishment would pay us a fee to register with the exchange. In return, we would offer access to partnership funds, which would not have to be paid back, rather than have them incur debt. A small fee would be charged to one who chooseth to invest funds with us. Our profits would be distributed in relation to one's share in the partnership."

After sitting a while and discussing other matters of trade, we rowed back across the lake. I thanked him for hearing me, and we set off on our separate ways. I went to Farad to discuss our industry and future plans for broadening the exchange.

"Prince, I come with an idea that should bring prosperity unimagined to the kingdom."

"Thou hast already done more than one hundred men to increase the wealth of the people. If thou possesest yet another idea that sheddeth more happiness upon them, I shall submit thee to the king for an honorary designation."

"I would be humbled of any such consideration, but I shall let you judge the merits of mine idea before any such honor be granted. We have encountered many merchants who have inquired of access to more gold in order to expand their trades. I propose to further extend the pooling of townspeople's funds to partnerships within the entire region, not just with the merchants of Solat. Tradesmen would share their profits with the people. It will create a vehicle for men of modest means to generate wealth, and merchants to expand business and grow profits while minimizing the burden of debt obligations. We could charge both merchants and townspeople for the right to partner through our exchange."

"Thy business savvy and philanthropic nature never cease to amaze me. Thou hast demonstrated wisdom in commerce unlike any man in record. I firmly believe this to be the most promising idea yet, for it enhanceth the lives of all who partake of it. We should begin its implementation posthaste," Farad declared with intense passion. Seeing his reaction to my theory generated in me a feeling of absolute contentment. That I could inspire such attitudes in men affected me deeply.

The prince and I quickly put our new plan into action. When the people understood the inherent risks involved in partnerships, our venture was well received. As it grew easier to obtain aid with the use of others' gold, more people opted to form their own businesses.

Over time, the region flourished as new trades were established. Men no longer struggled in search of labor; merchants were in search of men to fill new posts. Everyone was able to accumulate wealth and improve his lifestyle. Upon instilling these new forms of commerce into the regional culture, there was an overall feeling of fulfillment throughout the land.

Looking back at the forces that compelled me to start anew, I truly understood what it meant to gain insight from decimation. I became not dismayed by defeat, but rather created ways to improve my condition. Once the error of my ways underwent a thorough study, I was able to foster new ideas. I sought the companionship of those who would support me. The vision this association bore had become so powerful that it created a center of economic activity through which all men might prosper. Because mine efforts remained focused on creating value for others, my name became celebrated throughout the region.

* * *

The prentices were awed by the tale as they stood before the edifice to which the Baron brought them. As their eyes traveled upward, they saw an inscription that read, "The Qahhar Society of Alchemists." 'Twas in that moment the realization dawned upon them that they were standing on the very ground where the Baron's father perished in the original school. The Baron's accomplishments were so extraordinary, they could hardly wait to be the philanthropic magnates they desired to become. So inspired by his account, the Baron's pupils yearned to emulate his model, though they knew that much knowledge still needed to be acquired.

"Witness the clarity that is born from severe loss," the Baron proclaimed as he gazed at the sign bearing his father's name. "So, my wards, tell me what ye have learned today."

"That no man is born adept," Tunde asserted. "Only through struggle and repeated failure may one begin to control circumstance. Defeat teacheth lessons that may be learned solely through its occurrence; it aideth to redirect one's efforts to a more promising course. 'Tis through failure that man recognizeth his flaws that will lead him to become his ideal self."

"'Tis not one's failings alone that produce mastery of self," Mbolaji offered. "One must study the causes of such failure and apply new methods with persistence. Defeat doth not weaken a man of resolute will. The resistance he experienceth only serveth to aid in fulfilling his wishes."

"Students, ye should be aware that there will come a time when your foundations shall be tested with failure. When that time ariseth, ye shall determine if the principles on which ye stand are solid," the Baron warned. "Khaleef, thou art silent. Hast thou not taken away any message?"

There was a pregnant pause. Tunde and Mbolaji glanced at each other fretfully. Finally, Khaleef spake, "I have learned 'tis not glorious times by which a man should be judged, but rather by his response to defeat. That the wise do not becometh dejected, but strive harder with each setback, confident that victory is near. With all that failure seemeth to take away, it also planteth the seed of triumph. If one nurtureth it diligently, he will be able to look upon his past with laughter."

An obvious look of concern stretched across Khaleef's face

before he added, "Teacher, though we have consummate ambition, in hearing your tales I worry that we have not the quintessential ideas to match."

"Be not vexed, young one. Thou only hast doubt because thou hast not had enough failures to develop grand ideas. It took me years to make available such complicated schemes. I advise taking informed risks early, so that any possible collapse might happen quickly. One can learn from these delays and still have the time needed for recovery. Fear not failure, for it is necessary in gaining mastery of self. One who doth not fail maketh no attempts. Not to endeavor because of fear is the only true shame."

ALLIED EFFORT

The following morn, the pupils rose earlier than usual. As had become routine, they bathed and dressed, then made their way to the Knowledge Chamber. Due to their early arrival, they entered the study to find the Baron in the midst of daybreak meditation. The students stopped midentry and waited outside, careful not to disturb him. After a few moments, the Baron invited the three inside, then beckoned Wali to bring them sustenance.

"Master, hast ye been meditating upon your definite purpose?" Mbolaji queried.

"No, students, I was in counsel with mine alchemists," said the Baron.

"But, teacher, we see no others in your presence," Tunde countered, befuddled.

The Baron chortled and motioned for them to be seated.

"'Tis what the mind perceiveth that shall keep one paces ahead. 'Twill allow one to profit whilst mounting debts are incurred by those who discern not. One may avoid peril whilst others increase the possibility of becoming further entangled."

"Pardon mine ignorance, my lord," Mbolaji said.

"Thine apologies are not necessary. To leave something unquestioned is the purest display of ignorance. Thou shalt appreciate the value of alchemists completely by day's end."

Intrigued by the Baron's mysterious statement, the students hurriedly reached for fresh papyrus and quills to begin recording the wisdom key of the day.

"Allied effort is a major component to assure victory. It is divided into four sections: guidance, coalitions, the Alchemists Guild, and interactions of the cognizant and subconscious mind. In order to attain the unification of these elements, one must be willing to hold the aims of a group as his leading precedence. When gaining support, one needeth demonstrate the benefits of championing one's cause. Upon doing so, the people will support him. He whose ethical code fostereth collaborative efforts will not only accomplish his aims, but will find his life enriched due to this constructive approach.

"First, we shall examine the guidance between learner and counsel. Since ye are here with me, I know you to have some understanding of this concept. A mentor, if ye have elected properly, hath already walked the path ye seek to follow and made errors ye hope to avoid. He will have formed alliances ye shall seek to forge. Understand, even with the advisor's wealth of experience, paths will differ. Heed your tutor's wisdom and identify where it applieth throughout your individual course.

"Then, on the subject of coalitions, men well-suited for your situations are essential," the Baron continued. "They determine the nature of one's life. By forging such alliances, ye are exposed to knowledge and opportunity normally considered inaccessible. By introducing your associates to other competent men, ye shall be able to increase opportunities for success. What is more, these relationships will spawn innovative ideas that will change the way ye approach commerce. One who achieveth by organizing men's efforts will receive a more substantial reward than one who achieveth success through toil only.

"Next is the Alchemist Guild. This is a group of people who come together to achieve a common aim. Its synergy produceth collective thought that no single individual could devise alone. For this reason, the alchemists' strength are unmatched. 'Tis important that each member in the group possess an asset the others lack. By fashioning an Alchemists Guild in this manner, there will be no weak unit. Mind you, this assembly needeth not always be in physical form, it may also be derived from one's own imaginings. If every alchemist should focus upon achieving the same end in a perfect union, the way shall be cleared for the establishment of a collective mind. This group achieveth maximum effectiveness because each alchemist is willing to hold the group's shared objective above his personal interests.

"Cooperation between the cognizant and subconscious mind is most important," the Baron explained. "The recommendations of the subconscious are those that are drawn into reality. If one doth not deliberately suggest that which he desireth, he will become what others wish him to be. A wise man, therefore, intentionally useth his alert mind to protect his subconscious, only allowing ideas that will encourage him to achieve his aims."

* * *

Through my relationship with Prince Farad, I was finally able to receive the title due me by birthright. Father had endured hardship in hopes that I would not have to suffer the same; now his efforts were no longer in vain. Albeit the public knew not my real identity, the name by which I was known meant "He Who Helps." A member of the court trumpeted mine achievements from atop a turret in the king's palace so it could be heard throughout Solat. I had brought the region prosperity, and in doing so was now about to have my name . . . well . . . a name, attributed to royalty. It would be the second time in my family's history. I was certain that Father's tutelage played the foremost part in my successes. As I donned the required traditional vestments of bone white with purple and gold trim, my thoughts were interrupted by Farad. He entered my quarters to find me gazing out the window, lost in reminiscences of days past.

What would I have done without mine associates? If not for Prince Farad, I would not be standing here in the king's palace. However, I found myself conflicted about whether I should be receiving of such an honor. Whereas one king had taken Father's life for teaching the Laws of Gold, here was another bestowing honor upon me for imparting the very same.

Though Father was disenchanted with nobility, I saw the value of obtaining a noble title for myself; without it, I would not be able to help the people in the manner I desired. I was sure he would understand had he lived.

As I finished making ready my presentation for the ceremony, I remembered how Farad taught me to think as dexterously as he in business dealings. I had joined with a man who possessed all the necessary ability I lacked. He showed me how to circumvent common mistakes that merchants normally made, particularly those of managing gold poorly and careless record keeping. Financially, he warned against spreading assurance income too lean and overdrawing our emergency accounts. In the areas where I lacked ability, he supplied mastery.

Though Farad professed how I helped him find a righteous endeavor through my philanthropic activities, it was he who made them possible. Without his financial prowess and soundness of mind, never would I have been able to put nourishment in the starving mouths of my brethren. Never would I alone, have been able to create employment and motivate people to fashion their own ideals and value their livelihoods. We did this together using a collective mind. Farad, as well, would not have accomplished as much without my contribution, and I know he valueth our alliance justly. However, my gratitude toward him is unparalleled, for Farad facilitated the means to properly acquire wealth; through him I was able to realize my dream to teach the Laws of Gold.

Prince Farad asked, "Is anything the matter?"

"Just thinking back on our first venture together, is all. The events of the day are most overwhelming. To have finally realized everything I set out to accomplish amazeth me, truth be told. Ye hast done me a gracious service, and I am proud to have made your acquaintance. We have come a long way, no?"

"Aye, my friend, we have. Let us not think this journey done yet, however."

"Indeed not," I rejoined. "I have suffered the sting of loss enough to know I shan't want for her."

"Then it is agreed. May neither of our minds, nor those of our children unborn, worry should failure present itself again. If that time cometh, we will have tools on hand to remedy the pitfall, and can bequeath this knowledge to our offspring."

"From your lips to fruition. Pray tell, do they expect me now?"

"'Tis the reason I have come," Farad announced. "The king is not to be kept in wait."

"Let us not delay. Shall we?" I adjusted my robes once more and stepped down from my dressing pedestal. Farad signaled that the door be opened, and I was preceded by a dozen garrison. We marched throughout the kingdom, and all who were associated with the nobility of Solat saw my face. The grand courtyard where the ceremony was to take place was filled with the king's personal guard. Known as the Royal Knighthood, they were arranged by rank facing the king's immense throne of intricately carved ivory. The entire setting was blinding in its white splendor, from the white marble columns, floors, and walls, reflecting the brilliant rays of the daystar. White flower arrangements filled the air with scents of the fragrances that had brought me such acclaim. It was absolutely quiet in the courtyard, save for the sound of the clanging metal from the armored guards as they walked ahead of me. When we were within one hundred paces of the king, two mounted guards pulled on the reins of their cream-colored stallions. The beasts whinnied piercingly and reared up on their hind legs. Their hooves struck the marble with loud claps. 'Twas then mine escorts halted and parted on either side of the throne. They drew their scimitars above their heads to point them in my direction as I stood in the center. It was like standing under a roof of glinting metal.

The king spoke: "Initiate, thou hast made Solat quite prosperous. The ideals that have sprung from thee have made my coffers overflow. I shall henceforth acknowledge thy rightful noble position in these lands. Come forward and kneel before the throne." He rose from his ivory masterpiece and was approached by his son, Farad, who carried a polished scimitar with bejeweled hilt, resting on a white silken pillow. My body was atremble as I slowly came forward.

Pride exuded from mine every pore; I tried hard not to smile childishly as I genuflected at the bottom stair leading to the throne. Had I not been patient, certainly this day would not have arrived. Without persistence, life would carry little meaning as I passed each day listlessly. By not falling victim to stagnation, I was able to offer benefit that surpassed any man, regardless of his station.

The king, blade firm in his aging hands, expertly rent my garment on the right shoulder, drawing trickles of blood. It stung, but was far less painful than the time it took to effectuate its realization. "I now dub thee a noble of Solat. May all men regard thee as such."

The white cloth became crimson as it absorbed from my wound. I stood graciously, then bowed in gratitude. The king took his seat and his crier called out, "All rise and salute the Baron." Everyone rose as I took leave of the courtyard and entered a sea of people hailing my name. My scarlet badge of honor glowed amidst the pristine backdrop.

The next few days I spent in solitude. Again I visited the Vale of Oorjit and went to a secluded area where a cliff fell to deep blue waters and coral reefs. Questions of how I could continue to assist as many people as possible plagued my mind. Not being able to fully discuss mine ideas with the majority of individuals in my presence, as my character was too complex for the lives of most, I sought the understanding that introspection granted. By looking within myself for the proper answers to these pressing issues, I successfully made mine Alchemists Guild in my conscious mind. Nasir divulged this secret long ago, and I had been utilizing this skill with consistency when executing my life's plans. Having inner discussions aided in placing me on the right path. Where I faltered, my mental advisors presented rational resolutions.

This process also taught me that one can access creative thought by two means: by developing one's own ideas or by aligning oneself with men capable of doing so. I elected to benefit from both whenever possible by making use of fruitful thoughts and calling on specialists whose innovative abilities ran in countless directions.

To clear mine head of its clutter, I climbed a rock face one hundred hands high, then plunged into the cool liquid far below. This I had done on myriad occasions before in my youth, yet I found it much more rewarding at present. I concentrated on piercing the water instead of making a terrible splash, and inhaled deeply upon resurfacing.

These days of contemplation proved therapeutic. I realized whilst diving, 'twas Nasir's assistance that proved itself true when I needed it most. His counsel was certainly responsible for my praise thus far. Had it not been for his counsel, I would not have been able to progress in such quick time.

Then my thoughts turned to my trusted and loyal crew. As I, they had risen from naught, to become men of imagination. I made it my concern to find men capable of devising plans through which to procure mine aspirations. This proved wise. I observed in my dealings with those around me that each person was affiliated in some way with every other being. We were all connected as one powerful unit to help one another. I needed only a few contacts to arrange the attendance of anyone in the world. My chances only augmented the more associations I forged.

And then there was the importance that self-control taught me. Constantly being mindful of my thoughts during waking hours allotted mine imagination the creativity necessary while resting. Several of my best ideas were born from the fruits of the subconscious. Had I been more deliberate about what I was thinking in my developmental stages, perhaps I might not have fumbled so often.

One who uniteth the four pillars of Allied Effort with integrity shall find his house forever enduring.

* * *

The Baron chose to take his prentices to a sporting event that the whole territory had been eager to attend for several moons. They were seated on stone benches in a private section of the arena, with a perfect view of the playing field. The home team wore uniforms of red, and the visiting team was clad in blue. The game was Crosse, with teams of ten men each, in which a stone was carried, thrown, and caught with a long-handled stick having a triangular frame at one end with webbing in the angle. The objective was to launch the stone into a defended net on the opposing team's side of the field by any means necessary.

The blue team's strongman scored the bulk of their goals, yet was starting to show signs of weariness toward the close of the match. As he progressed toward his target, one red defender aimed to check his advance by attacking the trunk of his body. A second defender rushed him with his stick suspended in both hands to bar his advance midfield. In a brutal collision, the defenders converged, flipping their opponent head over heels. As the strongman crashed to the ground, the stone was freed, recovered by the red team, and passed upfield immediately toward the blue goal. After five passes of the stone, the red team scored its first and twentieth point to win, settling the rivalry. A glorious uproar came from the crowded arena as spectators threw flowers and small bits of colored paper onto the field. The sweaty home team bowed before all sides of the sports ground to thank their patrons. Then they shook hands to congratulate one another on a game well played.

The Baron flicked a piece of lint from the knee of his scarlet raiment.

"What hath been made evident from this day?"

"That a man may accomplish more with the aid of others than through individual efforts. Moreover, one should associate with men before needing their aid. There is no power that shall match a group of capable men who have subjugated their individual aims for one common cause. In doing so, one shall multiply the efforts of each man infinitely," answered Tunde.

"It is also essential to form associations with men of various means," answered Mbolaji. "'Tis prudent to surround oneself with talented minds specializing in every field in which one intendeth to operate. More important is to seek ways to empower all men, for if one is honest in his pursuits, he will not need to solicit their aid, they will offer it freely. By seeking to enable others, one will never lack opportunity. He shall be the one they first envision when any prospect should arise."

Khaleef added, "Mastery of self is key. To control cognizance, and thereby one's subconscious mind, is the clear mark of a successful individual. This ongoing practice only heighteneth the scope of one's notions."

"Ye have exhibited comprehension. Before rest tonight, record in your scrolls a list of every person ye know. Next, share your lists amongst one another. This shall be your foundation upon which ye might foster alliances. When these teachings are completely understood, establish and maintain contact with each person on the list. Seek to identify their needs and desires, and if ye find that two of your associates require similar assistance, pair them together and ye will have helped; in turn ye can expect higher gratification in the future. Also understand that upon befriending one man, ye align yourselves with his allies and the benefits they are able to offer. One should cast aside no man of positivity, no matter his standing. Those one least expects can have surprisingly well-connected friends."

After the crowds dissipated, they rose to leave. Whilst leaving the field, the Baron counseled, "When persons conjoin themselves in a harmonious effort, each in the group thereby multiplieth his ability to effect change. No man could bring about enduring results without the aid of another. To digress from unified endeavors hath destroyed more enterprises than any other reason.

"Take these decrees and reflect upon them. Embrace them as ye have done all others. Continue to repeat your definite purpose each morning and night, and envision how the men on your lists might aid you in reaching your aims."

COMPOUNDING

llow me to spin you scholars a fable of another sort . . .

Once there were three men: one we will call Knowledge, another, Time, and the last of them, Wealth. As they often did, on this day they began a debate on their own importance.

Time turned to Knowledge and voiced, "Without me, thou cannot reach thy full potential." Then, feeling rather significant, he turned to Wealth and taunted, "Thou wouldst not be allowed growth in mine absence."

Wealth responded with, "Devoid of my presence, thy days would be filled with hardship." And to Knowledge he added, "Our values compare not. I am demanded by all, yet held by few. Besides, supplied not with me, thou wouldst be left adrift."

Knowledge rebutted, "'Tis true, thou art held by but a few men, yet 'tis because they know not my name." Then he directed his attention to Time. "With a fair amount of prudence, I need thee all the less. Furthermore, lacking me, thou surely wouldst not exist."

A growing sense of indignation compelled Time to declare unto Wealth, "In a man's last days he would forsake thee for my companionship."

Wealth proclaimed to them both, "Revered am I by all men. Perhaps 'tis I, then, who am the true measure of each of you. I can obtain thee, Knowledge; what is more, I can conserve thee, Time. If neither of you have attained me, what then, makes you consequential?"

Knowledge asserted to the pair, "Without me, ye both would be squandered away. I too, am able to retain thee, Time. And still create thee, Wealth."

Time rebutted, "Perhaps. Yet without me, neither of you would even matter. A proper allocation of mine attributes has proved to increase you both."

Wealth saw the truth in Time's declaration and spake his changing heart. "I concede with thine insights, Time. With thee, I should require less of Knowledge to mature."

Knowledge turned to Wealth and added, "Indeed, my friend, Time speaketh accurately. With his aid, I would be certain to create thee in abundance, Wealth. Conversely, with thine aid, anything would be a possibility."

Scholars, one needn't argue their levels of superiority. 'Tis evident through this parable that success dependeth on one's ability to leverage the strengths of all three: Time, Wealth, and Knowledge. Their destinies are intertwined, making none less significant than the other.

* * *

"Nasir, thou hast imparted a lot of thy worldly wisdom upon me over the years. For this I am truly thankful," I said.

"Think nothing of it, friend. So long as thou appliest what thou hast learned, that is gratitude enough. An apt pupil I have found in thee, for I am impressed enormously by thine accomplishments, applying the teachings at every instance."

"I feel it only right and exact to share some of what I learned before developing an association with thee. Permit me to take time now to give an account once told me by Father when I was small, so that thou mightest understand the foundation I was left to cultivate. 'Tis only now I can recollect it, after having overcome so many obstacles."

"Please do not hesitate to expound upon what thou hast learned. Perhaps thou shalt teach me some profound lesson," Nasir jested when making the latter statement, or so it seemed.

"Once there were three fishermen—their names escape me at the moment. Father presented this account much better. I do recall their dominant features, however, which maketh the narrative credible. One was a cautious man. We shall call him Cansi for now. The second was ambitious in his pursuits, and we shall name him Egis. The third was a man recognized among his fellow fishmongers for his general wisdom on most topics of the day; quite the conversationalist he was. He will be called Glesne henceforth. Each earned three pieces of silver per week by selling his catch at the local market. Upon every week's end, they were forced to deal with the situation of allocating their earnings wisely. This was done in an attempt to satisfy their vast personal needs with a limited supply of funds.

"Cansi would apportion two silver pieces for his daily sustenance and one for the warranty of his fishing line, should it break. This particular allowance gave him the most comfort. He knew in the recesses of his mind that wealth never would be his fate with such an allocation; nonetheless, neither would he want for provisions. Thus, he was a content man.

"The second man, Egis, assigned two pieces of silver for nourishment and one to hold in savings each week, that he might eventually afford a second fishing line which would cost some twenty silver pieces. He felt the best way to improve his lot was to trap and sell more fish. Longer hours were required of him, but he hoped to reap heftier proceeds. Egis ran the risk of being forced to spend the larger part of his savings for another line if it were ever to break. Regardless, he was willing to place this wager. He was optimistic that within less than two seasons he might double his earnings.

"Glesne chose to spend his two customary silver pieces for food as did the others, but with the remaining one he invested in a trade that produced fishing lines. Each season, this establishment divided a sum of gold coins amongst its depositors, and he would receive a dividend proportionate to his investment. He was most certain that as his outlay increased, his dividend would augment equally. Glesne saw even the most minuscule amount of ownership as a better alternative to duress of any kind, and it was hence the method by which he chose to improve his lot. Willing to risk the possibility of his line breaking, he planned someday to enjoy ample wealth despite the consequences.

"Each of these fishermen chose to expose himself to perils of a different sort. Cansi risked earning an insufficient amount of silver for his efforts. His savings would be incapable of supporting him when he grew unable to fish in old age, the time when gold would be most in need. With no monetary backing to secure financial independence as an elderly man, his position was quite precarious. Perhaps his mental picture of the future was not farsighted enough to counter this detrimental outcome.

"Egis's chance of success was restricted. His earnings were solely dependent upon, and thereby limited to, himself. Because he was only one man, he could catch but so many fish. It did not matter how long Egis ventured down this path. His strategy created mental comfort for him, and his future would be more secure and restful than Cansi's. Sadly, though, he would never prosper.

"Last, there was Glesne, who took the hardest risk—standing, thus, to garner the greatest rewards. His peers referred to him as a sage, not because of his wisdom, but rather his foresight. If his strategy proved him wrong, he would face hardship, and his earnings would cease to grow. Hopefully, he would have stored enough away to rebuild in a timely fashion. However, if successful, his endeavor would allow him to experience a lack of restriction, rather than labor to an early demise, having acquired nothing but two stooped shoulders. In the end, Glesne might profit from his investment in the fishing trade and live the rest of his days in contentment.

"That narrative demonstrated to me that the choices of these three men were neither correct nor false, but instead were mere consequences to be mulled over. Father taught me it was best to examine life's choices before enacting them—that I must question whether my daily decisions mirrored those of Cansi, Egis, or Glesne, the sage. Through the telling of this anecdote, Father succeeded in educating me to fully understand the long-term consequences of mine actions."

Nasir cupped his chin in the hollow of one hand and the back of his head with the other. He twisted his head on its axis, cracking his neck first to the left and then to the right. It was a sharp crack that seemed far too loud for a man of Nasir's proportions. He shivered in delight at the sensation and collected himself. "A divine account, one containing some hard-learned truths and apparent life lessons. I understand why Qahhar recounted this tale to thee at a young age. A wise man himself, he wanted to impress upon thee the importance of thine actions before folly could take hold of thy conscience.

"Thou hast applied the ethics of his account suitably enough. Albeit thine earnings are not limited like those of the three fishermen, thy wealth hath afforded thee significant authority not only over circumstances having to deal with thyself, but also those that affect thy brethren. Thou shalt always be faced with satisfying limitless needs with seemingly inadequate resources, despite how multiplied thine holdings become. Wilt thou focus thine efforts on maintaining what thou hast already, immediately increasing thy lot, or wilt thou implement a completely different idea, one which may not disburse until thy progeny bear seed of their own, yet which will most likely require less physical toil?"

Needing not ponder Nasir's question overlong, for I deliberated much during my days of introspection in Oorjit, I answered in what seemed a rehearsed tone, "I have learned it best to divide mine efforts—and earnings more importantly—into three factions. First and most significant is to apportion funds that would provide for my needs through old age. After all, when one's back weakeneth from much duress and is of use no longer, one should have anticipated its oncoming exhaustion. 'Tis not as though an ailing backside never warneth of collapse, 'tis simply that one electeth to heed it not. I will dutifully attend to all warnings and distribute gold as I see fit.

"Subsequently, another portion will be designated for the efforts of increasing my takings from one phase of the moon to the next. This constant attempt will ensue for mere survival and will only be attempted when the first component hath been firmly secured. This process will prevent any misconduct on my part and will lead to the success of my future offspring. Transgressors who proceed without foresight will lose their posts, leading to most unsavory times.

"Last, when triumph is certain and mine earnings are sufficient enough to carry over to the next full lunar phase, I will enact a plan to accumulate a handsome fortune in one fell swoop, the better to aid in the advancement of the people. To make an effort in all three areas will allow me to rest peaceably as my monetary returns increase with a force of their own. One who is shrewd taketh careful strides, aware that he who prepareth for life thus might guarantee himself a place amongst the most respected authorities on gold."

A soft rustling sound fell upon mine ears from the north wind as it stirred a pile of leaves to Nasir's left, forming a funnel by his feet. They seemed to dance as they encircled each other, shifting positions to the tune of the currents. There was a pause in the conversation as the sudden miniature gale with all its natural beauty had taken us both unawares. Just as quickly as the display had come, the cyclone of leaves returned to the ground where their branches had released them to perish. I could only think they had resurrected themselves to give one last farewell by way of the wind, when before they were left to rot.

Nasir broke mine inward contemplation. After reviewing my solution to his question, hearing Father's tale and appreciating its moral, a desire grew in him to teach me yet more vital life lessons.

"I wish to give further surety to thy victory by sharing three types of depositors thou wilt certainly encounter along thy journey. The first we shall know as the Commoner. He will surround thee most days, defined as thy patrons and the public majority. These individuals can be approached for only a small leave, in lesser increments. One must remember that the Commoner feareth loss, having experienced its anguish numerous times in myriad varieties. Thus, even when thy words have proved their weight in gold, he shan't give unto thee much of his own, as he possesseth little to begin with.

"The second type we shall know as the Enterpriser. He is a trade owner, employed of his own wealth. He is usually in search of ventures that correlate to his personal aims. Aside from these dissimilarities, the Enterpriser is able to employ the Commoner, although the reverse is never true. The Enterpriser compensateth for loss with assurances, yet is still not removed from enduring physical toil. When producing transactions for his trade, he createth manual labor for himself and his employees during the course of his daily covenants. Due to his increased wealth, the Enterpriser is accessible for larger pledges than his predecessor, the Commoner, and in more frequent and augmented increments when deemed necessary.

"The third is the Alchemist, who fashioneth models of commerce and implements them successfully. His distinction lieth in his ability to grow wealth for those who lack the wherewithal to compound their funds at an equitable rate. His daily business plan taketh into consideration that the affluent invest whilst paupers consume. He then optimizes his takings by making available products and services to them both. The Enterpriser might find several ideas that the Alchemist createth to be of value to him and could learn from his expertise. The Enterpriser's and the Commoner's interactions with the Alchemist are limited to labor and the purchase of goods and services. The Alchemist putteth one under so much scrutiny that to trade with him, one need be recognized as an Alchemist as well. If he can be approached, one may solicit him for any sum.

"With a valiant effort, thou wilt surely divine what others are left blind to. As thy knowledge hath amplified by leaps and bounds, so shall thy wealth and that of thy children. Watching thy progression from thy beardless years till present, thou hast impressed upon me thy capability to accomplish plenty when observing good habits as taught. They have each compounded in turn to make a better man of thee. Thou hast invested wisely in knowledge, allowing thyself to accommodate more risk and to leverage thy resources. It hath offered relevant tools that will increase thy rates of return in a timelier manner."

As we strolled down the main road, we happened to see a public notice on the wall of a store in town. Whilst perusing the details of the sign, Nasir remarked on its contents. "If the burgeoning plague being spread by the Patlaanites of the north planneth to rear its head in these lands," he reasoned, "then any and all efforts will have been for naught. Health, once again, should reign high on one's list of priorities, even above gold."

Baffled by reading such disturbing news so fresh to mine eyes, I questioned whether mine health was kept in check and whether I had associated with persons carrying this mysterious epidemic. My world spun, setting upon me a feeling of vertigo I had never before experienced till then.

"What of this plague, Nasir? Until now, I have heard no word spoken, nor seen it writ."

Nasir's eyes widened with disbelief. He sighed heavily, then admonished, "I believe not that a man of thy standing be so ill-informed on the issues of the world. This seemeth out of joint with thy character. The story hath it that aboard a foreign vessel headed north to the Patlaan region, a trapper of boar meat took ill midvoyage. By the time they reached port three suns later, this tradesman had suffered an excruciating demise. It so happened that his lungs seemed to liquefy without explanation. Within a week's time, all those who traveled aboard the same ship perished, meeting a similar fate. If the Patlaanites are unable to be contained during this epidemic, the entire civilized region might be at risk. As yet there is no cure, and being savages themselves, the northerners' knowledge of medicinal antidotes is nonexistent. Hence, they raid surrounding territories in an attempt at survival. A cure must be created to oppose the contagion before it spreadeth to thee and thine."

My being went numb and a sudden tingling from deep within coursed through my veins. A light-headedness caused me to whirl, and I lost my footing momentarily. Nasir held me upright, then sat me down with caution. So many thoughts and questions ran through me that I experienced a fleeting lapse of self-control—at least, I thought it to be this. With this thought, my composure was restored.

"Something must be done."

Nasir concurred.

* * *

"Now ye see with what foundation my father, Qahhar, saw fit to arm me. Nasir's confirmation and further guidance spurred me forward. It instilled the motivation I am trying to impart to you in case any unforeseen plight might occur during your times of growth," the Baron declared to his learners as they passed the armed guards securing the royal courtyard in Solat.

There was a festive mood in the air. Nourishment was aplenty, and a variety of amusements was available for all who wished to partake of them. The Baron had brought the students to a celebration in honor of Farad, who was that eve to be endowed with his father's royal title. Entering his latter days, the king thought it wise to retire from his more active responsibilities and pass them on to his adept son. So as not to lose influence over his heir, the king would still be involved in matters of policy.

Smells of fowl roasting over open flames permeated the dense night air. The tune of a flute could be heard from afar as a charmer lured a hooded cobra from its woven basket. Jesters balanced on globes whilst performing acts of jugglery. Parting a crowd as they made their way to the ceremonial hall, the group witnessed men performing feats of strength, hurling enormous boulders and challenging the distance of one another's throws.

"I wish to acquaint you with Solat's new king so that ye might further understand the import of this day's teachings," the Baron announced. "Farad is the continuance of the benevolent philosophy passed on by his forefathers. Each generation was able to bequeath a newfound knowledge and wealth to its successor that aided in a rapid expansion of power throughout the territory. That influence meant the institution of policies that offered increasing opportunities and stimulated economic growth. With unique experiences lending additional wisdom to each king, Farad hath become the culmination of these attitudes. Such a compounding of efforts should be emulated if one wisheth a similar legacy. However, before I make the introduction, I would like to make sure ye understand this principle thoroughly. Tell me then, prentices, what hath this day's parables taught you, fiction or otherwise?"

Tunde started, "With repetition, thoughts and actions multiply. Implementing constructive habitual practices is to be considered a cornerstone to one's lifestyle. Poor habits develop at the same rate as their opposite, so it becometh increasingly important to ferret them out quickly. If this is not done, one shall confront beast rather than babe. 'Tis important to decide now what one desireth in order to use time advantageously. There may be no investment more important than that which one maketh in oneself."

"Mbolaji, what carrieth importance with thee?" the Baron asked.

"Dealing solely in events with a high probability of success, one is far more certain to assure his chances of victory," he rejoined. "In addition, it is imperative to select alternative gold-producing vehicles when the one currently in use achieveth not a rate of return favorable to meet one's goals in a timely manner. One must obtain an inflow of coins that surpasseth one's expenditures. This can be achieved in one of two ways, by bargaining numerous covenants that reap small amounts of gold, or by negotiating one agreement for a large amount. 'Tis also wise to exercise one's positive influence on others in order to further expedite the compounding effect."

"A most excellent observation, my lad."

"Never use mine own funds when attempting to compound, especially when lacking competence over the subject matter pursued," Khaleef chimed. "The fact that one is inexpert implieth that triumph is not secured. Along the same course, never solicit contributions from others when aligned not with people who possess mastery over the area of interest. Ye hast successfully taught that one should be moving farther away from physical labor in an effort to create takings based on resourcefulness."

"Impressive, my charges. Also, take with you that no effort shall go unreciprocated. The longer your compensation shall be deferred, the grander your reward shall be when it arriveth. Pleased am I of your understanding; therefore come with me to meet the king."

SUPREME PRINCIPLE TENTH

REQUITAL

The next day, Wali was ordered to summon the inquirers to the study, where the Baron patiently awaited their arrival. His lessons from the previous day had charged them with overabundant energy. This caused them to discuss what they learned amongst themselves till nearly sunup, while they should have had proper rest in preparation for the new day. Not saying a word, Wali knocked on their chamber door and flung it open. His entire being filled the doorway when he straddled the mouth of the room.

Khaleef bolted from his mat with a start. "Oh, my!" he lamented, and hastened Mbolaji and Tunde to rise and make ready.

Without delay they bathed and dressed, then rushed to greet the Baron. They entered with grim, apologetic looks painted across their faces.

"Good day, students," bellowed the Baron with a grave look of his own. Yet after one look in their repentant eyes, he softened. "No matter how eager ye are to converse after hours, and I do understand your zeal, ye must always be prompt. We have discussed this in talks prior. Let it not happen again."

"It will not, my lord," responded the three prentices in unison.

"Well rested or not, we shall proceed posthaste to recover the precious time lost. Agreed?"

"Yes, great benefactor," Tunde said. "We have scribed diligently upon our tablets and debated all our views earnestly. In so doing, we have taken notice of the effect your teachings have on our thoughts and how they have transformed our inner selves."

"I am glad to hear it. Your transformation has not gone overlooked on my part. Ye are all progressing tremendously, which is why the content of our meetings hath intensified. Hence, I would like to direct your attention to plans that shall instill the universal law that governeth interactions with others." The Baron pointed to a scaled rendering of the territory, with several refuges for waifs and strays spread throughout, which were to be constructed once the proper funds had been secured.

"'Tis mine intent," he avowed, "to build these harborages in the names of surrounding kings, to benefit those whom I was once like. Here they will be refined, have their basic needs provided for, and will become proficient in the teachings I have shared with you. The ideas of each child shall be cultivated to better the expectations of the people."

"How wilt ye implement this endeavor?" Mbolaji queried.

"I shall entreat the neighboring sovereigns by proving a benefit to their respective provinces. Albeit I could fund the operation with gold from mine own reserves in seeing this undertaking to its reality, I should like to alter the mindset of the ruling class, inciting them to action."

* * *

I called a meeting of my five original prentices at Farad's estate in Solat, for mine was then still under construction. The gathering was held in a room housing an aquarium that formed one of the four walls in the chamber. The tank was filled with the most beautiful sea creatures from all corners of the world. Never had any of us seen an aquatic habitat so immense, save the ocean herself. Considering the arid climate in which Solat was located, such a large reservoir of water could only be maintained by the wealthiest of royalty. Farad had done well for himself.

All that could be heard in the still, empty room were the swish of our robes and an occasional slide from our camel-skin sandals. Our voices echoed against the polished glass of the aquarium and the slick, cornflower-blue marble tiles.

"I have gathered you here today to discuss the state of affairs into which our territories have been thrust. Is anyone informed of the occurrences taking place in the Patlaan region?"

Rawan stepped forth. With a phlegmy cough, of which we all took note, he began, "Many have fallen victim to a most terrible pestilence that is sweeping the land. I fear I might have to cease operations in Kresan and move back south to avoid infection. I am glad ye hast called this meeting regarding this matter, for 'twas on my mind to ask one of you."

Prince Farad interrupted, "Kresan? Is that not some five days' south of the Patlaanites? I should think that far enough from danger."

"'Tis not far enough for my comfort," Rawan expressed with much conviction. "This is a serious problem occurring amidst the troglodytes, and I wish it not to become one amongst the civilized peoples." He coughed again, this time more violent than before.

Seeing his friend's condition, Jalaal reached into a sack tied to his waist and chose from one of several vials of liquid. He presented it to Rawan for immediate consumption.

"What dost thou give me, brother?"

"I too, am glad this forum hath been called. Whilst maintaining records of our business to the east, I have discovered that much of the flora used in our fragrant oils have curative purposes. This vial containeth one of mine antidotes for a cough such as yours."

Mine attention quickly perked at such information. "What sayest thou, Jalaal? Curative?"

"Indeed. I have kept reports of my findings over many moons and hundreds of various cases. Bodily ailments and other physical maladies of myriad forms I have all but cured with limited failure. I have prepared a scroll."

Jalaal offered a parchment from his sack and presented it to me. I unraveled it and found charts and pictograms describing the success and failure rates of his case studies. Further reading divulged what combinations of plant life were used, and in what dosages.

"When didst thou have the time to research all these methods?" I asked, truly taken aback at this turn of events.

"I began experimentation when we all parted to operate in different territories, ages ago now. 'Twas then I realized my definite purpose was to hone this craft in order to help others. I had hoped none of us would fall ill before I did so, in order that I might compile enough successful trials with as many different cases as I could treat. I dare not bring to my brothers thoughts unproved. What I hold here," he raised a glass vial filled with a greenish fluid, "is a concoction of one part eucica root mixed with two parts oxtoa flower. It hath healed four and sixty of the seven and sixty cases treated. It will minister to thy cough, Rawan. Of this I am fairly certain. If not this, then another. In any case, a remedy shall be found for thee."

Jalaal extended the vial once more to his ailing partner. Rawan accepted it graciously and took its contents forthwith. "When will the effects make themselves visible?"

"By the first brightening thine ailment shall be in remission. If not, I must begin anew with thee."

I was floored with the possibilities. "Dost thou mean to say that thou hast encountered individuals with symptoms akin to the plague of which we speak? Hast thou the countermeasure?"

"As yet, I do not. I wished to be certain that I had your blessing for such pursuits. 'Tis for that reason that the scroll, albeit unfinished, was prepared from inception."

"By all means," I cried, "if thy purpose in life is to heal others in this form, then now is the time to step forward and make it known. I come to my brethren to discuss how we might bring solace to our people, and a possible solution stands here in our midst." The rest of the group concurred wholeheartedly. "From this day forth, thou shalt have every resource necessary to find a cure for this disease. It should consume our every thought until the proper combination hath been achieved. Rawan will stay by thy side, Jalaal, as I wish his development to go monitored by thee. We shall share the responsibility of our operation in Kresan whilst Rawan improveth his health. As of now, the moon is half visible in the night sky. When it beginneth to show itself anew, we shall reconvene to discuss the progress made. Privy?"

The men were attentive and ready to perform. It reminded me of days past, when our purpose was merely to satiate the pangs of hunger that each of our bellies shared. For that reason solely we made and sold fragrant oil at one point.

Now it would mean life or death for multitudes. Once everything was settled and we all understood our plans, I left Farad's domain in somewhat lighter spirits, given the circumstances.

Just outside Solat's walls, I encountered Nasir, who seemed vexed at being ignored by a roadside merchant dealing in Trezaje, a game of chance, one I was unaware of Nasir to partake.

"And therein lies the problem with humanity today, sir!" The merchant still paid him no mind.

"Thine actions should be based upon truth and righteousness, not the slight of hand in which thou dealest."

No matter how fervently or loudly he bellowed, the dealer disregarded him. "Thine unmerited dealings will return to become thy fate."

Nasir turned to me, disgusted at such contemptible treatment. "Man is so easily corrupted," he spat. "Their thoughts turn their hearts rancid when consumed by vices such as this." He pointed to the swindle taking place. Every unsuspecting onlooker who participated in the vendor's game was duped by his ruse and left with emptied satchels.

"I can recall thy position on such encounters from lectures past." I began to recite verbatim, "'When speaking to a man, address him once. If he heedeth not thy words, attempt once more. If after the second turn he heedeth them not, communication through action is thine only recourse.'"

"Haunted by mine own utterances!" Nasir exclaimed. "Very well, then. On to more important issues. Away with this brute. Accompany me to the public gardens, wilt thou not?"

With that, we began to stroll in the direction of the gardens of Solat, sharing in a comfortable silence. 'Twas the type of hush reserved only for those who consider themselves to be close friends. "Farest thou well?" he finally questioned.

I told him of the discourse I had held with mine initial partners.

He responded justly, "Thou now wieldest a previously unimaginable power. The more a man liveth for others, the richer his life becometh. Having given of thyself, thou now expectest nothing in return. This is the quickest of paths toward wealth everlasting. Thou hast vanquished the enemies of thine innermost self and art now to be considered a man who embraceth his brother and careth for his troubles. However, do not embrace the despair of thy brethren, or 'twill most certainly become thine own. 'Tis a fine line when deciding upon to whom one might show compassion, yet be not eager to dole out judgment."

To which I reasoned, "Whether the transgression be effectuated by consideration or deed, 'tis implausible for me to wound my fellow man without harming mine own person. I will gain no less, even if my brethren should falter, for mine act of goodwill shall reflect positively upon me. Some might choose to deny what I am warranted for mine assistance, but none will be able to dispossess me of the recompense I will draw from my generosity. Others might assume they have wasted their humanitarian acts on those who neither appreciate nor requite them. However, I know that one reapeth benefits one hundred times greater than the act of kindness extended with this form of habitual practice."

"Moreover," Nasir added, "thou hast shown possession of an understanding of Qahhar's teachings that I am uncertain he himself ever exhibited. For thou now proposest to aid those to whom the general majority cast an ill glance. In so doing, thou hast rid thyself of any competitive inhibitions thou mightest have entertained. Burdening thyself with thoughts of preeminence over another is futile; history hath proved thus. Instead, thou chose to inspire, which always beareth the greater fruit. This premise should serve as the law by which thou governest the majority of the circumstances that befall thee. 'Tis an insufficient act to tithe gold when humanity is the real prescription to aid thy fellow man. True sacrifice, true deliverance, are only realized when empathy for another hath been felt intuitively."

I made sure Nasir realized that I fully understood his doctrine. Every so often I displayed certain body language to demonstrate my comprehension.

When reaching the public garden, Nasir determined it best to allow me freedom to meditate. 'Twas only he who realized the decisions left for me to make, and witnessed my mental exercises before they took form in reality. During mine introspection, I contemplated exactly how much in resources would be necessary to combat this developing scourge. It took not overlong to determine that the amount was more perhaps than the land allotted, for there was but so much foliage available. Furthermore, if I were to give away any remedy that Jalaal concocted free of payment, this, too, could very well cost more than I possessed. I dared not goad poverty, yet my position would be for naught if everyone around me were a potential threat to my well-being. I pondered the matter well into the day, yet was unable to find an answer.

Farad permitted the use of his fortress in Solat for the production of Jalaal's serums. Rawan, after one sunup, seemed restored, yet to be certain, Jalaal administered to him a second dosage of the green fluid he had consumed the day before. This time, there was no contesting its medicinal validity. Rawan covetously drank the liquid. We could not be certain he carried the epidemic in his veins, only that Jalaal seemed to have cured his ailment. Was this proof enough to gamble the lives of the townspeople who might fall ill? It was too soon to tell. Rawan was bedridden by order of Jalaal, and anyone within fifty paces had to cover his mouth with a fine cloth.

During the time of the plague's spread and the ongoing raids, the civilized lands had been divided. Those who believed that the Patlaanites might invade, thereby infecting their territory and pillaging its resources, moved their families to regions far west, near water. Others, who had yet to witness the extraordinary illnesses befall their own, stayed, choosing to live their lives unchanged.

Farad announced, "My men report a foreign increase the likes of which we have never seen. I have ordered a quarantine of all newcomers into Solat for a fortnight whilst we observe their physical states."

"Might I express mine interest in that post?" asked Jalaal. Without turning his attention from Rawan, whom he was tending, Jalaal inspected several points of interest on Rawan's body, carefully observing and recording his findings.

"Providence hath made for us a most fortuitous turn," Farad said. "If thou wouldst, please begin immediately. Do exercise great care, Jalaal, for what fate would befall us if thou fell ill thyself?"

Jalaal pointed to a neatly arranged box of scrolls. "I have pared down every step into simplified descriptions. No great feat will it prove to duplicate my processes. Where will infected subjects be held?"

"They will be isolated in the old stables. They have been unoccupied since the westerly section of the fortress was erected."

"That might not be the optimal location. Germs might remain from the horses that once resided there," Jalaal said.

Farad conceded to this thought, as this was not his area of expertise. "Well then, what dost thou propose, Jalaal?"

"I will have to ponder it a while. Let us begin, shall we?"

I was put in a position where, once again, the motivations of another had to be intertwined with mine in order to relieve people in need. 'Twas a place in which I was able to find comfort in knowing that the end result would be favorable. Conversely, present circumstances were different from my previous mission of bringing prosperity to my brethren in the form of material wealth. Here I was party to restoring their physical health—a prosperity of sorts, but uncharted territory nonetheless. Putting my trust in one who was instructed by mine hand, albeit he was a dear ally and worthy pupil, represented new waters into which I must tread. Our roles had been reversed; Jalaal was now mine instructor, and I his avid learner.

* * *

Wali had servants bring before the Baron pitchers filled with cool water from the nearby springs. The second footman served it to him in a goblet that had been chilled in advance. He drank copiously of its contents, as he was parched from retelling his chronicles to the three pupils. Their duties completed, the servants were dismissed and made their exit. The Baron cleared his throat.

"One cannot give oneself up to injurious conduct and not suffer a loss of one's own power. Likewise, 'tis an equal inconceivability to impart one's goodwill unto another without deriving benefit."

Tunde proposed, "'Tis no surprise that humanness is inclined to return a like gesture. No longer should others' lives be perceived as external to one's own, nor should one view one's existence as individual, for all our destinies are inextricably linked."

"By acting against my brother, I set in motion a negative

sequence of causalities that shall revisit me twofold," Mbolaji offered. "I will encourage him to enact revenge and weaken both our efforts, for they would have been better employed in more productive means. 'Twould prove nothing but the weakness of my character. By thinking ill of my brother I plant in my mind the seeds of doubt and fear, for just as I have unfairly criticized him, I shall encourage others to think the same negative words of me."

"Well said, mine acolyte," the Baron complimented him. "One who possesseth comprehension of this principle would sooner sully his resting place than indulge in untoward deeds, for he knoweth that such iniquity blemisheth one's standing, bringeth damnation of mind, and impedeth the realization of success." He took a sip of water from his goblet while Mbolaji took a mental note of this addition to his lesson. "Khaleef, thy thoughts?"

"Every exercise of the intellect hath an equivalent response that shall pose a challenge in consequence. One mayn't change the nature of this moral precept, but will find it best to conform to it accordingly. Its authority will bring a sense of consummation inaccessible without it."

The Baron stood from his regal chair upon hearing the declarations of his three avid pupils. He eyed them proudly, then placed his chalice on a side table. Wali had it removed upon noticing it. The disciples took their cue from the Baron and rose with their heads respectfully bowed.

"Raise your eyes to me, scholars, and mark my words onto your tablets straightaway." They obeyed, their black eyes glistening with tears unshed, so humbled were they, and appreciative of such a singular request.

"The means ye have used to implant your definite purpose is the same method by which requital takes hold. One's character is built or shattered by one's thoughts and deeds.

Each positive act reinforceth the good of your temperament. Contrarily, with each misdeed, ye instill its opposite. Pessimism shall leave an indelible mark upon you. When applying requital to your daily lives, all judgment levied against another shall be applied unto you. Show compassion and ye shall find the same benevolence returned. As ye learned, your being is magnetic, attracting in others that which ye exude. Despite all efforts, ye may not conceal your innate qualities.

"Censure not, lest ye be condemned. Malicious acts invite assaults on your personage. Live for others, and slander of your name will fall upon deaf ears, for ever increased will be the number of men who will come to your defense. Deeper will their compassion be should ye falter, thus more certain will your confidence be in difficult times.

"Since the beginning there have been overlords and serfs. Some attained their position by circumstance, others by volition. Hold not contempt for the overlord who wieldeth onerous power in fear of his own inadequacies, nor disdain for the serf who aspireth not for freedom. The two are unenlightened to the true repressive force that acteth as their restraint.

"Unbeknownst to the serf, 'tis his own suppression of will that leaveth him tethered. He findeth comfort in his subjugator's hand. The bound man seeketh not the impelling force from within that would motivate a change in his condition; he shall languish each of his days until he findeth such an impetus.

"The overlord is oblivious to the understanding that his tyranny only weakeneth his character. With each brutal act, he buildeth a wall of ill will around himself and will find subversion at every turn. What prudent man would create an antagonist unnecessarily? Is not a friend of greater comfort in times of despair than an adversary?

"Trust in this principle and it shall never abandon you," the Baron concluded. "Reflect upon and embrace this virtue as ye have all others. Proud am I of your retention. Continue to ruminate over what ye have learned, only be not forgetful of appropriate rest and promptness come sunup. Refreshed, we shall reconvene upon the morrow."

I AM

eeling completely out of mine element whilst contemplating the most difficult situation in which I had yet been placed, I met with Nasir. He led me through the gates of mine estate to a side garden that even I had not chanced to visit until then. My mind raced through memories of the plans for its construction, but I could not remember seeing any courtyard.

Once there, I regarded its tall and lush, expertly manicured hedges, as well as the inviting scent of the honey blossoms enclosed within them. Nasir directed mine eyes to the center of the private garden where a most unique sculpture lay. The sun blazed on a table of petrified wood. Intricate carvings were set in the almost tiger-like pattern of its grain. Upon closer scrutiny, I realized that these etchings depicted a story that seemed to chronicle my flirtations with opulence.

Mine eyes glanced over the pictorials and missed not the smallest detail. The craftsmanship compelled me to draw a similarity between the illustrations and all I had experienced with Nasir these past years. The story of my life unfolded to every side of the table save one, which ran smooth and untouched for the remainder. Feeling bereft, I hoped to find a glimpse of my closing stages; this chronicle had yet to be completed.

"Am I to be a stranger in mine own surroundings? What is this place, and how dost thou know of it before I? And this artwork? Tell me of its maker so that I might query his ambition and knowledge of my life."

"Whatever leadeth thee to believe 'tis thine history engraved here?" Nasir skirted. "Moreover, 'twould not be the first time my grasp of information hath superseded thine. Are these the matters that concern thee most?"

I hesitated and looked once again upon the carvings. Where just before there was no mistaking the face to be a small replica of mine own, the more I searched the characters, the more resemblance to Nasir they seemed to bear. Was it Nasir's tale, after all? How could that be? Only seconds before, these same faces and incidents reminded me of myself.

"Either mine eyes deceive me, or there lurks an evil in that piece. What hast thou at work here, Nasir?"

"The issue of superior import is however it will all end. Hast thou overlooked this?"

"I am still uncertain if it is truly my life being recounted here, or thine own."

With this admission, Nasir's temper grew fierce, slow to rise, yet quick to smolder. "I came to thee long ago when mine aid was most necessary for thine advancement. Thou sought externally for validation during those times. Thou already knew what must be done, the circumstances and people to avoid. Under extreme conditions the mind reacteth in a manner fitting for one to succeed. I was spawned in response to thine ominous predicament. All this time I have merely projected thy thoughts and said what thou knowest to be truth in thine heart.

"Mine existence is the way to examine thyself objectively as would any impartial observer. I have served as mentor, the portrayal of thine imminent self. All the wiser, thou thought it best to be counseled by the greatest man thou knew—the man thou chose to become."

Mystified by such a pronouncement, I was without coherence.

"So thou art but a figment? An apparition of sorts?" I reached out and poked Nasir on the shoulder to see if my finger might slip through, as if trying to pierce a cloud. Sure enough, my touch proved him to be as present on his spot as I was on mine.

Offended by my gesture, he spewed, "Thou concentratest on all the wrong things! Sometimes I believe thee to know nothing whatsoever! How many more scrolls must thou read?

"Thy focus determineth what becometh authentic! In knowing this, thou shouldst realize that one inviteth what one is, rather than what one desireth. Dost thou understand now why I came to thee?"

This was too much. My mouth went dry and I felt a stinging sensation from behind my nose that traveled to the backs of mine eyes. Not only had my mind been afflicted, my body was suggesting that it too, could not bear the encumbrance of Nasir's good sooth.

Was I out of sorts completely? Nasir was mine imminent self? Why had he a different name from mine? Everything in me rebelled. I wondered what I had gotten myself into.

"Bombast! Thou cannot lead me to believe that I have

sent myself a future representation of mine own likeness through all logical forms of time and space to guide me. I have placed all my trust in thy judgment, Nasir! I can only re-call the situations in which we publicly spake with each other. Meanest thou that I was perceived to be conversing alone, as would a madman? This cannot be so. I deny this falsehood with all my strength."

"Those of us who share enlightenment are not hindered by the barriers imposed on the mind by outside influences. I have been trying to impress upon thee the importance of being able to transcend the social mores thou hast been sub-jected to throughout thine existence. Nevertheless, thou still concentratest on the inconsequential.

"'Tis best to be forward-thinking whilst not wasting the present," Nasir continued. "In spite of everything, thou must learn to resolve the inner conflicts that oppose thine aims. Apply thy mind rather than simply regard it as a storehouse for facts. Embracing this concept will unleash a spring of understanding gained only by the contents already possessed within thy reasoning. One cannot explain the pleasurable sounds of music to one incapable of hearing."

* * *

'Twas early morn when Wali, on horseback, guided the stu-dents, who were on foot, through the dense mist of first light. A eucica tree alongside an untilled field served as their bea-con. The rich black soil they plodded through to arrive at their landmark looked to be awaiting irrigation for the next season of planting. Formerly used to grow wheat, the land was being prepared to cultivate various hybrids of exotic flowers that the Baron had invented. Cutting through the thick vapor, a figure gallantly rode to meet them. This was the unmistakable silhouette of the Baron. The lush earth swallowed his steed's hooves with every purposeful stride. He slowed his approach as he neared, and alighted from his mount to join them under the tree. Wali kept a watch over the surrounding area as the Baron began his address.

"Today will be the last time that we gather. This dawn, I have elected to impress upon you a final lesson. Pray, let the significance of its teaching feed you in a most transcendental way, to serve as your bread, so that no other shall be required. Not unlike many things, it beginneth with one's mind rather than one's actions.

"In understanding this principle, ye shall comprehend the totality of your power, for with it ye shall understand how a man is able to create his destiny. Ye shall become the force that directs Fate, rather than the object swayed by her whims and caprices."

"We have been taught from youth that an unseen hand determineth our destiny," Tunde avowed. "Are we to understand that the mind is that unseen hand?"

The Baron clarified, "Each of the previous tenets hath offered but a glimpse into the possible, but 'tis through this one that understanding the true significance of all thoughts and actions shall make itself known. Ye shall appreciate why each thought must stem from integrity, and each action be utilized productively, for both carry a power that may not be undone and will spark a chain reaction with which ye will one day be challenged. A man with understanding of this law would sooner ingest poison than live in disaccord with it."

"Instructor," Mbolaji humbly beseeched, "ye spake of other principles with vast power. Doth this one hold a superior force? If so, need we command only it?"

"Indeed not. This lesson, which we shall term "I Am," will provide you a context with which to realize all things.

'Twill demonstrate why a wise man striveth to live in accordance with the first ten. Yes, men have found happiness and fortune without this knowledge. However, 'tis only with its application that one can reach his apex. A scant percentage turneth inward for deliverance when 'tis made known that the Great Kingdom spoken of in scrolls is contained within self. If ye truly possess this understanding, it shall become the impetus for all your actions. By making yourselves the object of intense study, ye shall discover the source of all things and will seek not outside your person. Seeking externally will only hinder you from knowing your true self."

"We are very excited to learn the profound effects of 'I Am,'" rejoined Khaleef.

"I had heard rumors of men who possessed such understanding," Tunde added, "but who when questioned, concealed this wisdom."

"Thy words convey much truth. A limited number of men enjoy command of 'I Am,' but a sword hath been placed above their heads to prevent its utterance. If its revelation were ever to be spoken, their heads would certainly be taken," replied the Baron. He said this with a firmness that startled his listeners.

"So why is it ye mayest reveal this teaching?" Mbolaji stammered.

"'Tis because I am a descendant of the originators of this teaching, not of the faction that wisheth its suppression. For centuries, 'I Am' was an entire scroll lost to the very masses that needed it most. 'Twas known only by a few and held closely in order to exploit the poor and unlearned. These disingenuous tyrants enslaved the people with debt and poisoned their thoughts, leading them to lives of misinformation, ill health, and struggle. The contents of this scroll have been lost too long and must now be disclosed to the masses.

No longer shall happiness elude them, for 'tis with this knowledge that they may change their condition. As the proper selection of herbs mayeth cure the ills of the body, this teaching cureth maladies of the intellect."

* * *

The morn after Farad's men realized the volume of foreign entrants in Solat, the prince met me and my brothers in his steam chamber. An impressive construction, the circular room was tiled in white stone, with a small pit of boiling water in its center. We were seated on white stone benches attached to the wall, making the recessed cauldron the focal point of the unique room. Every so often he added eucalyptus oil to the bubbling pot. We marveled as it emitted exhilarating clouds of steam that engulfed us, impairing our visibility. The heat caused us to perspire liberally; however, I found it quite soothing. 'Twas a highly curious innovation, and my mind could not refrain from wandering. How did the water remain at a constant boil? And by what means did the smoke escape, for 'twas not being let into the space?

In that room, when the novelty of the steam chamber wore off and we were able to center our thoughts on more pressing matters, our small assembly proposed several ideas regarding how to properly handle the forthcoming days. It was decided that inspections of the Solatians would be held in tents that Farad would pitch in the main square of the town. The Royal Knighthood was to be at Jalaal's disposal to assist him in maintaining order as he administered the serum to all suspected of carrying the disease.

Rawan, who had been required to keep his mouth covered with a filtering cloth, sounded much better at our meeting than he did earlier, which gave us all courage. He needed not clear his throat when he expressed, "There is another aspect of this matter we must address this day as well, brethren."

"What troubleth thee, Rawan?" I inquired.

"Solat is not an appropriate location to stand against the Patlaanites should they attempt to invade. 'Tis far better to engage in conflict on the territory of the enemy as opposed to thine own. This we cannot do, for the Patlaan region is infested with their disease. Bearing this in mind, I feel it only right that we position ourselves in Kresan, a halfway point and a means by which we may halt their advance. That region's denizens and topography are familiar to me. This would prove a more legitimate effort to keep the troglodytes from encroaching on this great empire."

An epiphany was revealed to Farad upon hearing Rawan's proposition. "The king of Kresan, Pordimus, hath been a dear ally for many years. I will send word asking permission to allow the Royal Knighthood entrance to assist in the fortification of his province."

"How will we administer the serum?" one of my brothers asked. "Should we give barrels of it to the infected?"

Jalaal refuted, "They cannot dispense the antidote in that form. The Patlaanites have no concept of a civilized existence, let alone how one would properly dole out the remedy. The Patlaanites tread upon all fours and rear their offspring among wild animals. They treat each other as equals until one group hungers for the other's flesh. We would have to fashion the cure to be consumed by utilizing an inconspicuous method, a basic animal function even they could comprehend."

I added, "Would the serum lose potency when combined with other properties or heated by flame?"

After a brief pause, Jalaal reflected, "I think not. Why, my lord, what hast ye in mind?"

The idea rolled off my tongue as easily as it was conceived. "Mightn't we bake a bread for the primitives to ingest, thereby curing them unawares?"

Farad interjected with a most valid point, "What if they engorge themselves?"

"My studies show that the effects of an overdose are drowsiness and temporary loss of memory, all dependent upon the actual amount ingested," Jalaal responded.

"We have no reason to believe they will not invade once their strength is restored," Suma, the quietest and youngest of our group, interposed. "We might be aiding in our own undoing. Is there any way to make them docile, Jalaal?" I was quite surprised to hear him speak. I assumed this to be a clear indication of the fervor bubbling under the stoic composures of my brethren toward this mission. I smiled in his direction and remembered days when he followed mine instructions blindly. It now seemed that this project had forced him to come into his own. He noticed the pride in mine eyes and sat erect.

"Art thou suggesting that I add another component to the serum? Or might we try to civilize the Patlaanites?" Jalaal turned to me. "This is not my field of expertise, my lord."

"Nor is it mine, brother," I quickly admitted.

The prince interjected, "When I was young, my forebear told of a prominent sage who ventured into the caves in order to humanize the brutes, how he followed the confining, acclivitous trench along the extensive series of fortifications that had been erected to keep them from molesting civilization. I learned how the Patlaanites were exiled from society to become family with the wild beasts. He recounted how the sage circumnavigated massive barriers of stone reinforced with iron meant to impede travel to the northern region. Our sentinels found his aide at the gates soon after, unconscious and missing an appendage. Once he came to, his report detailed of the brave man's demise at the hand of those savages. He had been completely devoured." Farad poured some more oil in the boiling water.

This added yet another dimension to our predicament. Civilizing the Patlaanites might prove too difficult an undertaking. 'Twas better to concentrate our efforts on the task at hand than to spread ourselves too thin.

"There is not enough time to experiment with the serum by trying to add a drugging effect," Jalaal said. "Should we try to scare them into a retreat? Have we no weapons to leave them ill-prepared?"

"They attack civilized nations with much success. I would assume them to be familiar with all methods of war, regardless of their rusticity," said Rawan.

"Perhaps they will think to save the clan left behind," Jalaal thought aloud.

Suma rationalized, "Perhaps their people are no more. This is proving to be quite a crisis, brothers."

"In crisis lies opportunity. We must take a more tactical approach and make their weaknesses our strengths. Let us use their ignorance as our weapon." 'Twas then in that steamy chamber that I devised a thorough plan that I imparted in detail to mine adherents. Everyone agreed that it was the most comprehensive strategy thus far. This compelled us to act immediately.

"Pordimus, good friend!" Farad exclaimed upon entering the king's main hall in Kresan.

"Ah, good Prince," Pordimus greeted. "How wonderful to set eyes upon thee after so long. Farest thou well?"

"I am well, yes. However, as per the message I sent you regarding the political state of our federation and the imminent arrival of our foe, there is much to discuss."

"Indeed. My kingdom awaits thy decision. Thou hast

mine ear and the aid of my men. Come into my private quarters where we might discuss at length thy proposal."

The sun rose on the horizon, uncovering the expanse of land that was Kresan. From the watchtower, a sentry witnessed one of our scouts riding hurriedly from his northern post. From my ready position to the left of both King Pordimus and Prince Farad, in a wagon drawn by six workhorses, I suggested that Pordimus give the command to proceed. His order was repeated down a trail that extended five hundred wagons, each filled with loaves of serum-treated bread. My brethren were responsible both for the rear and for keeping our convoy in tight formation. This was critical toward achieving our planned success.

We rode out to meet the scout who described all he had seen. Coming from the north were tens of thousands of Patlaanites on foot, some fifteen thousand paces near. The moment of our encounter was fast upon us, causing me to pose another course, to which the king readily agreed. He gave the order to advance.

There they were, a gray mass of sickly, haggard people. As we turned to advance northward, Solatian and Kresanite soldiers began tossing loaves at the sick, whilst archers, poised at the ready, held the troglodytes at bay. We pressed more aggressively than before to arrive at our desired position on their eastern flank. The strategy worked well, and the idea to conceal the antidote in the loaves proved excellent; they recognized that bread was for consumption, and voraciously partook of it. Perhaps during their invasions of other peoples they had tasted this staple. Twice the order had to be given to dispense the bread at a faster rate and at a farther distance, to reach them all. I grew uncertain as to whether or not we had prepared enough.

The swarms seemed without end. The Patlaanites were trampling each other as they attacked the bread to hoard self-ishly. 'Twas not long before we witnessed the effects of their gluttony by way of the soporific properties of the serum. No more than five thousand paces from our starting point, the invaders began showing signs of sluggishness and exhaustion. One by one they collapsed to dreamless sleep where they stood. 'Twould be presumed later that their malnourishment aided in the remedy's fast action.

Mission accomplished, a final order was given to ride north of our sleeping enemy and empty our carts of the remaining loaves, leaving a trail of bread in the direction they had come. Once every cart had been depleted, we fell back to Kresan, past the mounds of loudly snoring troglodytes.

We arranged ourselves well outside the gates of the territory in case any of us carried infection. Jalaal had everyone who had been exposed to the Patlaanites inoculated to keep the germ from spreading. I remained on edge until word was received from our scouts of their whereabouts. The survey team reported their slumber continued until the following day. Signs of forgetfulness were evident as they consumed the loaves with resumed vigor once more on their way back to Patlaan. Those left behind, upon realizing their numbers decreasing, followed suit and made their way toward the caves they called home. On the third sunup, no sign of them remained. We were convinced that they had indeed been confined. The garrison of Kresan was assigned the duty of blocking any means of their return. Our plan had worked; we had repressed the incursion of the barbarous swarm.

That evening, Kresanites and Solatians rejoiced and partook of splendid festivities in the main square of Pordimus's kingdom. All my brothers had distinctions added to their marks, Jalaal receiving the highest accreditation of all for his pioneering efforts in creating the serum that kept us from peril.

My brothers and I founded an apothecary as a result of our increased fame. Farad found pleasure in venturing into new opportunities centering not on gold, but on creating benefit for our people. My name was mentioned alongside the most learned sages in the scrolls of our history. Life turned out well.

* * *

The Baron folded his hands on his lap and stared into the eyes of his learners with a barely visible smile of contentment at the close of his tale.

"Your lessons are now ended. If ye shall recall only one thing, although I am certain ye have retained most of everything imparted these last few days, it should be that ye are the ones who control your destiny. There is no magical force regulating your existence, 'tis the thoughts and actions contained within that serve that purpose. Know and respect their might, for they have the power either to yield incredible aid or to disrupt your life.

"Superstitions will misguide you, diluting your force. Heed them not. Your mind is the source from which your outlook is drawn. Some men hear these words and regard them as rhetoric. They assume that because they have heard these teachings in part, they also live them. Do not confuse knowledge with understanding; for the latter to be true, application of these teachings must be evident. This step is the easiest to overlook. I may pass knowledge unto you, but 'tis your decision whether to act upon it.

"Make choices anew based on this vision. Quest neither

for gold nor for the power it bringeth, but for mastery of self. Once this hath been accomplished, create value for others. One is far more capable in this manner, for vainglory only leadeth one astray in serving others. Subjugate your conceit, and be pure in your intentions when helping your brethren. Ye shall never worry over wealth, peace, nor happiness.

"If a man achieveth not success, it is for one of two reasons: either he doth not know the methods by which to accomplish his aims, or he is afraid of the struggle to unleash his own power. One of those reasons hath now been eliminated for you, my pupils. 'Tis your duty to abolish the other. Ye have learned techniques whereby one might properly fashion thought and shield the mind from negative influences. Use these methods to share your vision with the rest of the world. Share your aims with the influential people in your arsenal and allow them to observe the growth of your person. This strategy will provide them hope. Show them how to create the opportunities that will permit them to live as they desire."

Each learner indicated that this request would be fully performed. Khaleef chose to speak. "Instructor, ye hast shifted our world and viewpoints; we will never be the same. We leave you today forever armed with the understanding that the mind is a tool used to shape the dispositions, circumstances, and fortunes of others. That a man is built up or taken down of his own accord, and hath no one but himself to hold accountable for either outcome. Aware of the dangers of not filtering with the conscious all that is allowed to touch the subconscious mind, we now know how to act every passing day."

"Deep into the night we have discussed our toils in searching for thorough understanding, and now 'tis finally ours to cherish," added Mbolaji. "We take with us that the further we search outside ourselves, the more truth will elude us. Long have we striven for this insight. Because of you, we need search no more."

Tunde said, "I have learned that one is drawn both to his fears and to his dreams, and that a man's state is the present value of his thoughts. His ideas fashion him into what he desireth. Even in a debilitated capacity, man is the overseer of his domain. Accepting this concept hath allowed me to understand that perception will equal one's reality. As a king guardeth his coffers from thieves, I must guard my mind from negativity in similar kind. No amount of gold shall ever find security in mine hands if my mind is not cognizant of the influence that others exert."

"Very true, Tunde. Men, if able, will have thee believe mysteries. Tend to your mind as would a gardener till the rich soil of this field that stretcheth before us. Dig out unconstructiveness in order to cultivate your positive thoughts without the hindrance of such weeds as negative influence or doubt, much like what hath been done for the exotic flowers that will be planted here. Speak 'I Am' with conviction, and what followeth shall create your existence. If ye embrace these teachings, they will protect you with equal force."

At the finish of his statement, the Baron motioned to Wali who continued to keep watch behind them. They exchanged conspiratorial glances, and Wali rode off toward the stables. The Baron redirected his attention to his guests, revealing nothing of what had just transpired.

"Young brothers, let us follow Wali's path on foot. We will meet him soon enough."

They walked alongside the empty field. "I am anxious to start this new journey, I must admit," Khaleef began. "My footing is sure to be strong after this fortifying education."

For a moment, the Baron was silent, for he always chose his words with utmost care. "If one heedeth not a potentially hazardous matter when life seemeth to be presenting one with no bitterness, it will prove far more difficult to overcome with the passage of time. The same is true of victory; it is to be prepared for when resistance is scant."

"Similar to what happened to you when the Patlaanites were threatening to pose a problem," Tunde observed. "Ye confronted a unique dilemma without letting it deter you or the assurance of your contemporaries. When 'tis known that one is causing his own intimidation, thus hindering his progress, one will become more steadfast. The only way to conquer trepidation is to recognize that one hath the ability to move through it. One cannot evade fear."

"Precisely," the Baron agreed. "Questioning the mind's power is analogous to doubting your ability to accomplish a task only because it hath yet gone undone. If ye were to tell an unenlightened man that his intellect is all he needeth seek, he would deny your charge. Alas, the masses remain sheltered from this fact and possess not its understanding. Thorough acquaintance with one's mind shall offer up solutions to the incomprehensible. Ye now possess the knowledge required to utilize your life force in total."

They arrived at the stables where the Baron's staff had assembled for the students' departure. Three stable hands came from the stalls, leading three magnificent horses the color of black ink, each with a newly polished leather saddle. The stable hands presented the reins of the horses to Tunde, Mbolaji, and Khaleef respectively, as parting gifts. The students were humbled at this presentation.

"These steeds will serve as symbols of my teachings. Whereas ye walked here slowly to undertake such an arduous journey in search of knowledge, these horses will speed your way toward your next destination, that of success. A man cannot consider himself learned without experiencing life. I have witnessed much transformation in you already and know ye will travel a long way. I am certain your progress will be far-reaching."

The students dropped their reins to embrace the Baron. They thanked him for his time, hospitality, and willingness to enlighten them. Each assured him that he would spread these teachings so that the fruits of his generosity would be multiplied. The young men gathered their scrolls and departed on their steeds, renewed and with a deep sense of purpose, equipped to start their lives anew.

'n

THE BARON SOLUTION

A Roadmap to Wealth, Power, and Success

Learn why top business leaders, sales professionals, and entrepreneurs hail *The Baron Son* as a remarkable breakthrough guide to self-mastery, leadership, and wealth-building. If you are ready to move your life or business to the next level, the following services and workshops will help you master the book's compelling principles.

Leadership Workshops, Coaching, and Consulting

Our leadership services focus on how to increase your personal impact and create sustained value for your organization, staff, customers, and shareholders. Learn to develop vision and enhance your leadership style to influence others and secure their support.

Sales Workshops/Sales Team Development

Discover winning strategies to increase business referrals and effectively sell to decision makers at all levels of an organization. Learn to create synergy, increase cross-selling opportunities, and find new markets to sell your products and services.

Direct Selling Workshops

Empower your representatives with new knowledge and skills crucial to building a solid base of customers and down-line representatives. Learn the Baron's inspired approach for motivating others to take meaningful actions that will help their businesses thrive.

Wealth-Building Workshops

Learn the Baron's unique *Four Portfolio* approach and other valuable strategies for building wealth when you have limited ideas, time, and money. Learn to leverage key resources and people to help you create wealth.

To register or get more information on these and other workshops, please visit:

WWW.BARONSERIES.COM

*Custom programs available for individuals and companies

Your Trusted Source for
Wealth and Business Education

Patterson, Davis, and Patton (PDP) have developed a powerful line of books, CDs, videos, and services to help ensure your business and personal success. We would love to hear your comments and testimonials on how our offerings have benefited you. To learn more about our tools and special events, and to share your success stories, please visit:

WWW.BARONSERIES.COM

Register online to win a free audio CD version of *The Baron Son*.
Audio CDs are also available for purchase wherever audio books are sold.

To order our products online, visit www.baronseries.com
Special promotions and volume and other discounts available